A BROCADE PILLOW

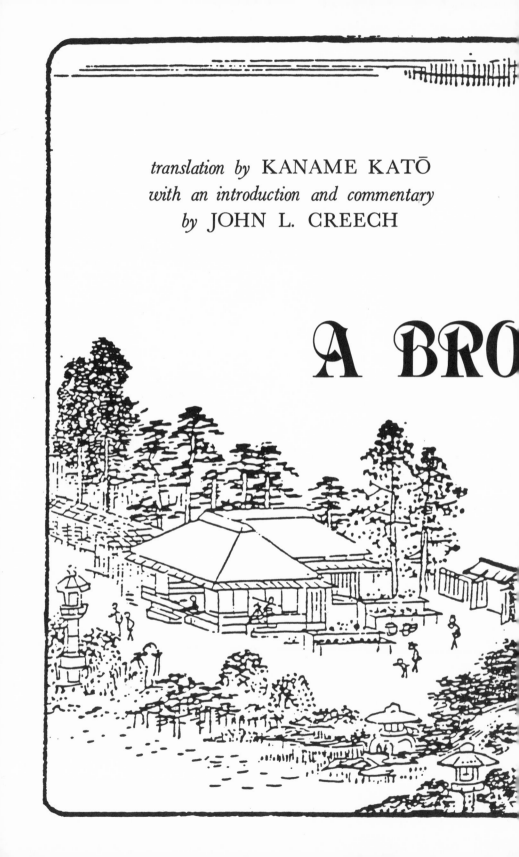

translation by KANAME KATŌ
with an introduction and commentary
by JOHN L. CREECH

A BRO

ITŌ IHEI

CADE PILLOW

Azaleas of Old Japan

New York · WEATHERHILL · *Tokyo*

A Brocade Pillow is a translation of *Kinshū Makura* and is based on the 1976 reprint supervised by Yōtarō Tsukamoto and sponsored by the Satsuki Society of Japan. The title page illustration shows Itō Ihei's home and nursery in the Somei District of Tokyo and is reproduced with the permission of the Satsuki Society.

First edition, 1984

Published by John Weatherhill, Inc., of New York and Tokyo, with editorial offices at 7-6-13 Roppongi, Minato-ku, Tokyo 106, Japan. Protected by copyright under the terms of the International Copyright Union; all rights reserved. Printed and first published in Japan.

Library of Congress Cataloging in Publication Data: Itō, Ihē, 17th cent. / A brocade pillow. / Translation of: Kinshū makura. / 1. Azalea—Varieties. 2. Azalea—Early works to 1800. I. Creech, John L. II. Title. / SB413.A918513   1983   635.9'3362   83-23571 / ISBN 0-8348-0191-4

Contents

Color plates appear following page 2

Preface

The horticultural literature of the Western world scarcely touches upon the accounts of Japanese azalea growers. This is unfortunate, especially when one considers that the majority of the garden azaleas in the West are of Japanese origin. It was in an attempt to rectify this failing that Kaname Katō and I set ourselves to the task of producing an English edition of *Kinshū Makura,* the five-volume classical Japanese treatise on azaleas by Itō Ihei.

Kaname Katō has had a long and successful career in horticulture. It was he who first guided me, in 1955, through the fabulous array of Japanese azaleas as we journeyed together to the nursery centers of Angyo and Utsunomiya. As a result of his considerable knowledge, I was able to introduce collections of many species and new cultivars into the United States during my years as a horticulturist for the United States Department of Agriculture. These introductions are documented in the *Plant Inventories* issued by the USDA and also in *The Azalea Book* (1965) by Frederick R. Lee.

In 1974, during a visit to Japan, Katō led me to the National Diet Library to show me an original copy of *Kinshū Makura.* Katō was at that time busy as a coauthor of the forthcoming Japanese facsimile edition of the work, and he was enthusiastic about its importance and interest. The Japanese edition was supervised by Professor Yōtarō Tsukamoto, and several prominent horticulturists assisted: Katō, Masaaki Kunishige, Yoshitarō Ogawa, Yasuhiko Maejima, and Hisaburō Oshima. The Japanese Satsuki Society published their work in 1976 in an effort to make the rare wood-block-printed original available to the many azalea growers in Japan today.

Katō and I became convinced that our colleagues in the West also deserved access to this unique work and decided to embark on our translation. Over the next several years, Katō labored over the difficult task of translating the seventeenth-century text into an English draft. It was then my delightful role to read and revise Katō's work, and to compose comments that relate the original to our contemporary knowledge of azaleas. Thus we arrived at the text as it appears here. We believe it is a faithful rendition of Itō's remarkable and often difficult work.

A Brocade Pillow, as we decided to call it in English, presents the translator with numerous perplexing choices. Most of these are concerned with names—names of azalea varieties, names of flower forms and patterns, and names of colors. Several modern Japanese azalea varieties are cultivated in the West, and the most widespread current practice favors calling them by their Japanese names. We have followed this course for modern varieties. On the other hand, much of the charm and interest of Itō's work is lost unless we know that "Ōmu" means "cockatoo" and "Ukigumo" means "drifting clouds." Itō frequently refers to the meaning of a variety's name in his description, and the Western reader is handicapped unless he has an idea of what each name means.

In this translation, the meanings of old varietal names are supplied in parentheses following the Japanese names—in the headings of the azalea descriptions only. Two exceptions should be noted. First, the names of several azalea varieties are indecipherable; in these cases, "name obscure" appears in parentheses. Second, just as in the West, many varieties are named after the locale in which they are grown or a place with which they are historically or fancifully associated. If an azalea is named after a place, no translation is supplied, since any would be redundant. Only if the place is of special significance or interest is it mentioned in the subsequent comment.

Word division of the names is another thorny problem, given the agglutinative nature of Japanese. Names have been divided to help the Western reader identify semantic components whenever possible. Hyphens separate prefixes that indicate size: Ō- (large), Chū- (medium-sized), and Ko- (small).

The translation remains faithful to Itō's complicated terminology for color and flower form. The inconsistencies that remain are Itō's, and they serve to demonstrate that the need he felt to standardize terms was a real and pressing one. Major discrepancies— between an azalea's name and description, or between its description and the illustration, for example—are noted in the comments. In spite of Itō's attempt to standardize the terms he used, the reader will encounter a great many synonyms for such forms as hose-in-hose and double flowers.

Romanization of the seventeenth-century names follows the conventions of modern Japanese pronunciation. The commentary to the 1976 Japanese facsimile edition has served as a useful guide in this matter. Japanese words are italicized throughout except for proper nouns, "satsuki," "tsutsuji," and words that appear in *Webster's Third New International Dictionary.*

The original sequence of entries is preserved, for the most part, in the English edition; occasionally minor alterations have been made for mechanical reasons, but care has been taken not to disrupt or falsify the continuity of the Japanese text. The illustrations have been reduced by twenty percent.

The authors wish to acknowledge the collaboration of Jeffrey Hunter. Initially editorial supervisor, he became intimately involved in the historical and factual facets of the translation. We are also indebted to the Japanese Satsuki Society for the use of the illustrative material from the facsimile edition, and to the American Rhododendron Society for their support. The Japan Foundation is acknowledged for its financial assistance, which permitted me to travel to Japan for studies of early Japanese horticultural literature.

I would personally like to express thanks to Professors Y. Tsukamoto and M. Kunishige for the close collaboration I have enjoyed with them over some twenty-five years, and to the many other horticulturists, botanists, and nurserymen of Japan who have given

generously of their time and expertise, contributing to my understanding of Japan. Finally, this preface would not be complete if
it did not include my wife, Amy, who stood by for the many
months I was overseas on collecting trips and other explorations
during the years I have spent adding new plants to cultivation in
the United States.

John L. Creech

Introduction

For anyone who admires azaleas, *A Brocade Pillow* is an essential reference. Written in 1692 by Itō Ihei, a Japanese nurseryman, it was the first monograph on azaleas either in Japan or elsewhere. Itō's work provides us with an understanding of the extent to which the early Japanese knew their wild azalea species and how thoroughly they were able to ennoble these magnificent plants over a comparatively short period of time. In addition, *A Brocade Pillow* is important to the botanist because it documents the early cultivation of the Japanese azalea species and records the existence of Korean species in cultivation in Japan that were not known to the Western world until some two hundred years later.

One can only be awed by the sophisticated level of azalea culture that existed in the Edo period (1615–1867). It is doubtful that there are any objectives pursued by modern azalea breeders that were not taken into consideration by these pioneer azalea developers, who produced selections that have not been duplicated since. Curiously, it was only the simpler forms of these azaleas that reached Europe during the centuries following the appearance of *A Brocade Pillow*. Some azaleas did make their way to Europe during the eighteenth and nineteenth centuries to become the basis of the Belgian forcing azaleas, which were later introduced to America, where they became known as the "Southern Indica" azaleas. It was not until the twentieth century that Kurume azaleas were introduced to the West, and satsuki azaleas did not reach the United States until Benjamin Y. Morrison of the USDA acquired a collection in 1938 and 1939 under the misnomer

"Chugai azaleas." Similarly, the Hirado azaleas were unknown to us until collections were obtained by Creech during a collecting trip to Hirado Island in 1961. The Miyama Kirishima azaleas described in *A Brocade Pillow* came to our attention only in the last decade, when Creech and Sylvester G. March assembled a collection of forty-eight cultivars during their 1976 exploration to Japan for the U.S. National Arboretum. Yet every one of these groups was represented in cultivation at the time of *A Brocade Pillow*'s publication, though perhaps not always with the group names later assigned to them. Likewise, most of the species not described botanically until many decades later were already being grown in the early Edo period. The history of how these various azaleas reached our gardens is thoroughly covered in Lee's *Azalea Book,* and further background material seems unnecessary here. It is more enlightening to discuss the setting in which the writing of *A Brocade Pillow* took place.

Western nations first paid serious attention to Japan during the last half of the sixteenth century, when missionaries and Portuguese, Spanish, Dutch, and English trading companies began to arrive. The ultimate result of this initial forceful foreign entry, when Japan was little prepared for reciprocal exchanges, was one of suspicion and fear, with the consequence that by 1639 Japan's rulers had closed her doors through a series of seclusion edicts. Only the Dutch were allowed to remain, and they were relegated to a strictly controlled role, restricted to the island of Deshima in Nagasaki harbor. For the next 270 years, until the fall of the military government and the restoration of imperial rule in 1868, Japan remained a hermit empire. It was, as Itō says in his introduction, a time of peace—as well as of industrious self-examination. One result of the seclusion policy was an appraisal of the social order, the arts, science, domestic policies, and agriculture, including a thorough evaluation of the natural resources of the islands. This period is often known, in fact, as the "natural history period." After ten centuries of Chinese instruction in the use of plants in medicine and industry as well as the gardening arts, the Japanese had developed a broad base of traditional Chinese

xii

botanical knowledge. It was now time to direct this stock of wisdom to the natural richness of the Japanese archipelago. Here was a flora endowed with over five thousand species of higher plants, offering a remarkable variety of sources for medicines, foods, and industrial products. These centuries of seclusion and study must have been an exciting time for Japanese naturalists.

Ornamentals were not overlooked, and many of the feudal nobility developed an avid interest in their cultivation. Societies soon sprang up for the culture of azaleas, chrysanthemums, iris, peonies, and even genera of obscure plants such as *Ardisia, Psilotum, Rohdea,* and *Selaginella.* Variegated forms of many plants were perpetuated, including both native and introduced species. *Rhapis* palms were introduced from Southeast Asia in the early 1600s and enhanced by variegated and other forms that can still be found in quantity in Japanese nursery markets today. Along with plant collecting, exhibitions of cultivated varieties became popular, and, in the case of chrysanthemums, great shows at which up to eight hundred varieties were exhibited occurred in Kyoto and Tokyo as early as 1715. Elaborate cases for transporting flowers safely to exhibitions are illustrated in early horticultural books. These activities spurred a boom in horticultural publishing, and numerous gardening books ranging from simple illustrated pamphlets to multivolume editions appeared. Between 1681, when the first horticultural book, the *Flower-Bed Classification (Kadan Kō-moku),* appeared and the beginning of the Meiji era in 1868, more than one hundred horticultural books were published. In addition, some fifty books on flower arranging alone appeared. This energy and enthusiasm characterized the horticultural scene at the time of the writing of *A Brocade Pillow.*

Itō's purpose in writing *A Brocade Pillow* was to provide an illustrated description of the azaleas in cultivation and to correct some of the confusion caused by name duplication. Of the 332 azaleas he described, 171 belong to the tsutsuji group and 161 to the satsuki group, encompassing fifteen species—as best we can reckon from these early Japanese descriptions, of course. Two other ericaceous plants are described: *Enkianthus campanulatus* and

Menziesia ciliicalyx; and one other family member: *Daphne odora.* The reason for their inclusion is not explained.

The azalea descriptions are almost entirely of the flowers and, occasionally, the leaves. Plant habit, or mode of growth, is not mentioned. Itō developed a coding system to reflect flowering time, the basic means for dividing azaleas into tsutsuji and satsuki. It is the first and only time that such a technique appears in the old Japanese horticultural literature. Itō also employed a standardized terminology for flower patterns. A few of these terms have crept into modern usage, but generally horticulturists, Japanese or Western, do not describe flower-color patterns in such detail today. Varieties which were especially suited to flower arranging are so noted. Synonyms are listed for varieties known by more than one name.

Itō's descriptions of azaleas provide a rather clear picture of those on which the early Japanese relied mainly—when we can determine the parents and species of the variety under discussion. That picture has changed little to the present and it is not likely that there will be any significant additions to it. Among the tsutsuji group, *Rhododendron kaempferi, R. kiusianum, R. sataense, R. macrosepalum,* and *R.* × *mucronatum* were the main breeding parents from Japan proper. But it should be noted that *R.* × *mucronatum* was probably a natural hybrid between *R. macrosepalum* and *R. ripense. Rhododendren scabrum* from the Ryukyu Islands and *R. yedoense* var. *poukhanense* from Korea were also of importance. The small-flowered species, *R. serpyllifolium, R. tosaense,* and *R. tschonoskii,* were also in cultivation but have never figured in azalea improvement. No evergreen azaleas from China or Taiwan were cultivated, although some Japanese horticulturists suggest that *R. simsii* may have been introduced from China to Hirado Island.

Itō includes the yellow form of the deciduous azalea *R. japonicum* with the tsutsuji azaleas. Its appearance in *A Brocade Pillow* demonstrates that *R. japonicum* and its yellow form were in cultivation at the time of the German physician and scientist Engelbert Kaempfer's visit to Japan (1690–92), a point disputed by E.H. Wilson and A. Rehder in *A Monograph of Azalea* (1921). There

appears to be a distinct relationship between the color forms of
R. japonicum and hardiness, borne out by their patterns of distribution. The yellow and orange color forms are found predominantly on the southern islands of Kyushu and Shikoku, gradually disappearing among colonies farther north in Honshu until, at the terminus of distribution at Mt. Hakkōda in Aomori, the colonies are uniformly red. These are said to be the hardiest. Likewise, the tender *R. molle,* which is pure yellow, occurs only in the warm parts of eastern China. Another interesting fact relating to color is that Japanese nurserymen have learned to segregate yellow seedlings from red ones by vegetative characters long before they reach flowering age. They have observed that plants with red leaf-tip glands and with leaves which turn purple in autumn will be red flowered, while those with green leaf-tip glands and with leaves that remain green until they drop in autumn will be yellow flowered. The early Edo horticulturists were equally observant and quickly associated *R. japonicum* with its Chinese relative *R. molle* because both have the same poisonous properties, knowledge of the latter having been acquired from Chinese herbals. It was probably its herbal uses that first stimulated the cultivation of *R. japonicum* rather than its garden merits. *Rhododendron japonicum* is not used extensively in Japanese gardens.

Two other deciduous azaleas were in cultivation: *R. dilatatum* and *R. schlippenbachii,* the Korean Royal azalea. The latter carried the name "Kurofune," meaning "black ship," probably because of the Chinese ship by which it was introduced to Japan. It was highly prized from early times by the Japanese.

For the most part, the azaleas described by Itō are still in cultivation in Japan today and are also grown by American breeders in the form of numerous hybrid races. Of the two Japanese azalea groups, the tsutsuji are the more familiar to American gardeners because they are the first to flower, have such brilliant colors, and are easy to cultivate. They fall into two main groups, those stemming from the complex of *R. kaempferi, R. kiusianum,* and *R. sataense* —best represented by the Kurume azaleas—and those derived from the Ryukyu group, largely based on *R. macrosepalum, R.* ×

mucronatum, and *R. scabrum*, represented by such historic azaleas as Akebono, Ō-Murasaki, and Shiro Tae, as well as the large group of Hirado azaleas.

The Kirishima azalea, which is employed by Itō as a standard for the tsutsuji group, is somewhat of a puzzle. It has sometimes been referred to as "*R. obtusum*," but no azalea by that name exists in the wild. From its name, one would assume that Kirishima came from the mountains of that name near Kagoshima in Kyushu. But neither *R. kaempferi* nor *R. kiusianum*, which occur in the Kirishima Mountains, correspond exactly to the habit of Kirishima as described by Itō. This suggests that Kirishima was most likely derived from *R. sataense*, which grows on Takatōge, a small mountain near the port of Tarumizu. The habit and flower characters of the Kurume azaleas suggest that they, too, are derived from this wild azalea, with infusions from *R. kaempferi* and *R. kiusianum*.

The second group of Japanese azaleas is the satsuki, Japan's most precious garden offering to the West. The precise origins of the satsuki are obscure, but the two late-blooming species from southern Japan, *R. indicum* and *R. eriocarpum* (which Itō includes in the tsutsuji volumes), are the most obvious parents. Even so, direct crosses between these two species do not yield anything like the typical satsuki azalea. The Matsushima variety was used by Itō as the standard for satsuki azaleas. In addition to being the name of a specific cultivar, "Matsushima" was a general term to describe striped cultivars of satsuki. Westerners are most familiar with the satsuki as a pot plant for bonsai in Japan. American gardeners, of course, have relegated the satsuki to the garden in order to extend the sequence of bloom. Two types of satsuki are grown in Japan, however, the large-flowered bonsai type and a type widely used as a landscape specimen, either grown naturally or sheared into dense mounds. Trained in this manner, it resembles sheared boxwood or Japanese holly, but has the added quality of fine purple foliage color in winter. When viewed across a dormant *Zoysia* lawn in winter, mature bushes resemble large stones. In one nursery area of Japan, near the city of Tsu, Mie Prefecture, the

xvi

horticulture industry is largely based on the production of this type of satsuki, and locally the plant is called "Mie Satsuki." In the United States the Mie type is still not generally available. Itō calls this type of satsuki *"magaki,"* or "hedge" satsuki, and includes several varieties in *A Brocade Pillow.*

There are a number of conclusions about azalea development that can be drawn from *A Brocade Pillow,* and these are discussed in the specific comments on each volume, but they are worth summarizing here. The early Japanese were interested, just as we are today, in azaleas that flowered in both spring and fall. They also used azaleas in flower arranging and looked for types suitable for various positions in arrangements. The *koshimino,* or skirt, type, completely unknown in the Western world, was popular at the time and was considered an especially delicate selection. It has since lost its appeal, and the hose-in-hose type, which is a somewhat similar form and far more attractive, has replaced it. The reader will find that the early Japanese horticulturist, like his modern counterpart, had definite preferences and pronounced favorites; in the last volume there are listings of the azaleas that Itō considered to be the best. It is also amusing to note that in discussing propagation he alludes to the use of softwood cuttings but prefers to keep his exact method a secret.

A final conclusion about the development of azaleas described in *A Brocade Pillow* is that the process of the creation and propagation of such a wide variety of azaleas occurred over a relatively short time span. Although some of Itō's entries were "prized from earlier times," the author states that the best ones were recent developments. This sudden "azalea boom" probably spanned no more than fifty years. A similar pattern of development for the evergreen hybrids occurred in the United States. Except for the azaleas grown in southern gardens and Kurume azaleas grown as greenhouse plants, azaleas were uncommon as garden plants in cities like Washington, D.C. as recently as the 1930s. It is strange that azaleas were so slow in attaining the garden popularity they currently enjoy. A number of horticulturists visited Japan after the Meiji Restoration in 1868 and sent home all sorts of interesting plants. It is possible that since many of them were from the Northeastern states, they did not consider azaleas to be hardy. But one nurseryman, Louis Boehmer, opened an export nursery in Yokohama in 1882 and shipped vast numbers of plants to America and Europe over the following twenty-five years. His catalogue of 1903 offered azaleas in several varieties, including red, orange, and yellow forms of *R. japonicum*.

Azalea development really began in the late 1930s when Morrison initiated the Glenn Dale azalea project and Joseph Gable, of Stewartstown, Pennsylvania, undertook efforts to produce new hardy azaleas. These American pioneer breeders stimulated a number of breeders into action during the next forty years, many of whom based their hybrids on the creations of Morrison and Gable. Nevertheless, with the exception of *R. yedoense* var. *poukhanense* from Korea, which Gable used for hardiness, and *R. simsii* from China, which Morrison used for earliness and flower quality, American breeders have relied on exactly the same materials as the early Japanese breeders. Only recently has Polly Hill of Wilmington, Delaware, incorporated *R. nakaharai* from Taiwan for dwarfness.

A Brocade Pillow is an outstanding product of an exciting era of azalea history. Japanese breeders made a profound contribution to our gardens with the exquisite azaleas they created. They gave us the basis of a significant horticultural industry, which would not have evolved so rapidly without their pioneering efforts. This work is a treasure in the literature of azaleas and a useful guide to the modern azalea breeder. The reader is encouraged to enjoy, and perhaps follow, the advice that Itō offers in his postscript: "It is the beauty of the view, they say, that makes us, 'beneath the cherry blossoms, forget about returning home.' In these five volumes the shapes of flowers are illustrated and their colors described so that those who plant tsutsuji can walk among their flower beds and, observing their plants, identify them by name using this book, giving them pleasure even after the blossoms have fallen. As the delights of the four seasons unfold, leave behind all troubles and find yourself at peace, and the jeweled tree of the Buddha's enlightenment will take root, as you forget, indeed, to return to this fleeting world."

About the Author

Itō Ihei (his exact dates of birth and death are unknown) was a gardener and, later, a nurseryman in the early Edo period. Because of his great knowledge of azaleas, he was known as Kirishima-ya, or "Mr. Kirishima"—Kirishima being one of the most popular azalea types of the day. He lived in the Somei District (present-day Komagome, Toshima Ward) in Edo, Japan's capital, during the latter half of the seventeenth century. His family was of the peasant class and had resided in Somei, a major horticultural center, for generations. When the demand for garden plants to landscape the castle gardens of Edo increased, the Itō family began to specialize in ornamental plants and gained a considerable reputation as gardeners.

In this fashion Itō came to the attention of the feudal lord Tōdō Takahisa and was employed to plant and maintain his castle grounds in Somei. Itō gained access to and expertise in the cultivation of a broad array of ornamentals through his work for Tōdō, as it was the custom in feudal Japanese gardens to regularly renew the plantings in order to maintain the original character of the landscape. Also through his work, Itō acquired an extensive collection of azaleas, so many that he became an azalea authority. To have assembled the array of types described in *A Brocade Pillow* was a remarkable feat, even by today's standards. We can assume that during the process of developing his collection, Itō encountered the problems of proliferating synonyms and wrongly named plants that still plague us today. This must have prompted him to establish a standard system for describing azaleas and then use that system to describe the varieties in cultivation at the time. A most impressive result of his efforts was the creation of the coding system to distinguish flowering seasons of satsuki and tsutsuji that appears in *A Brocade Pillow*. This makes Itō's work exceptionally useful and different from any other works of the period. No other horticultural book for the next two centuries incorporates such an essential technique.

In addition to *A Brocade Pillow*, Itō Ihei wrote a general horticultural text, *The Silk and Soil Flower Bed* (*Kadan Chikinsho*), which was later expanded by his son Masatake. Masatake, also known as Itō Ihei IV, was to become even more famous than his father and, because of his numerous writings, was granted the special honor of visiting the shogun's famous Fukiage Goen garden of Edo castle.

We are indebted to Itō Ihei for his remarkable contribution to azalea literature—the preparation of a text that would be useful almost three hundred years later, not only in his homeland, but wherever azaleas are cultivated and enjoyed.

A BROCADE PILLOW

A colony of R. kiusianum, *the Miyama Kirishima azalea, growing on a mountainside at Ōnamidake, Kagoshima Prefecture, Kyushu.*

A closer view of the flowers of R. kiusianum. *This species together with* R. kaempferi *and* R. sataense *are the main parents of the Kurume azaleas.*

The koshimino, or "skirt," of a Kurume azalea from Kurume City, Kyushu. This structure was highly prized during Itō's time, but is rarely seen today.

Rhododendron kaempferi, *Kaempfer's azalea, in full bloom on Sakurajima, in Kagoshima Bay, Kyushu.*

A planting of Kurume azaleas at the Kurume Horticultural Research Station, showing the range of color variation.

A close-up of a salmon-flowered specimen of R. sataense *from Mt. Takatōge, near Tarumizu in Kyushu, showing clustered blossoms.*

Amagasa, a typical large-flowered satsuki cultivated as a bonsai in Japan, was introduced
into the United States by Creech and is available
in U.S. nurseries.

This bonsai specimen of the Banka variety
is a fine example of the variability of flower
color in the satsuki known in Japan today as
sakiwake, or "mixed flowering."

A close-up of the pink-tinged white
flowers of R. eriocarpum growing at
sea level on the island of Kuchierabu,
off the southern coast of Kyushu. This
species and R. indicum are the parents
of the satsuki azaleas.

A fine example of the hedge-type satsuki R. indicum *at Mt. Hakone, Kanagawa Prefecture. Satsuki hedges are commonly sheared into such stone-shaped mounds in Japan.*

Dramatic color variation in R. japonicum *is linked to range. The yellow form* (upper left) *is from southern Kyushu. Mixed colonies of yellow and orange flowering plants* (lower left) *are also found on Kyushu, as are more distinctly orange forms* (upper right). *Colonies at the northern limit of the range of* R. japonicum *at Mt. Hakkōda, Aomori Prefecture, on the island of Honshu, are vermillion* (lower right).

This cultivated specimen of R. scabrum *from Kago-shima, Kyushu, is a fine example of a blotched flower. A deep flush of color extends from each flower's throat.*

From a specimen of R. macrosepalum *growing on Mt. Horei near Kyoto, these flowers are described by Itō as "dappled" (kanoko).*

Introduction

Our land flourishes in this long age of peace. People live in ease and enjoy the delights of the four seasons, admiring the beauty of the flowers that thrive in our gracious climate. Over many years in this glorious period, I have collected tsutsuji and satsuki azaleas, the number of varieties increasing year by year until they now number three hundred.

In this book I have illustrated the various flower shapes and sizes, described their colors, indicated whether they are early, mid-season, or late blooming, and discussed the proper time for grafting and making cuttings.

When I stay at home and admire my flowers, the bare room in which I live becomes, for a moment, a fairy castle. As I gaze at the blossoms, my head pillowed on my arm, I feel as if I am resting in a brocade bed, and so I have called this book *A Brocade Pillow*.

Because different names are often used for the same plant by different shops and peddlers, in this book I have illustrated flower shapes and described their color patterns for identification purposes. I have also indicated the times at which different varieties bloom, for the convenience of growers who may graft several varieties onto one stock. If flowers on the same stock bloom both early and late, the resulting plant will be unsightly. Grafting methods for tsutsuji and satsuki azaleas are illustrated, and the appropriate season for grafting indicated. Likewise, there are several illustrations showing the methods for making cuttings, preparing the rooting medium, selecting cuttings, and planting cuttings, and these topics as well as watering are discussed [in Volume Five]. The mixing of potting soil and proper amounts of fertilizer are also explained. When a variety has two or more names, the synonyms are included. Varieties suitable for formal flower arranging are noted.

Flowering Season*

○ This symbol indicates early-flowering varieties, which bloom at approximately the spring equinox [March 21st].

■ This symbol indicates midseason varieties, which bloom thirty days after the spring equinox, at the same time as the Kirishima azalea.

▲ This symbol indicates late-blooming varieties. These belong to the tsutsuji group and flower later than the Kirishima azalea but earlier than the satsuki group. As a result they are called *ai no mono* (middle group), meaning that they flower between the tsutsuji and the satsuki groups.

Spring-blooming varieties are usually classified in the tsutsuji group, while those flowering in early summer are usually classified in the satsuki group, but there are, in fact, spring-blooming satsuki, and they are listed in the satsuki volumes [IV, V] in this work. There are also summer-blooming tsutsuji, and these are described in detail in the tsutsuji volumes [I, II, III].

*[For several varieties Itō neglects to provide code symbols for the season of bloom, though he usually notes the flowering period in his text. These varieties are indicated by an asterisk (✱)—ed.]

Flower Size

Because in the following volumes flowers are identified as large, medium, or small, sample flowers of these sizes are illustrated here.

TA RIN (Very Large Flower). Flowers of approximately this size are identified as very large flowers.

DAI RIN (Large Flower). Flowers of this size are smaller than the very large flower and larger than the medium flower. They are indicated by the character *dai* (大, large), while the very large flower is distinguished by the character *ta* (太, great or very large).

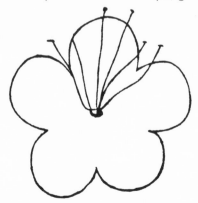

Chū Rin (Medium Flower). Flowers of approximately the size of the illustration are known as medium-sized flowers.

Shō Rin (Small Flowers). Flowers of this size are identified as small flowers.

Shō Rin (Very Small Flower). Flowers of this size are even smaller than the small flower, and are represented by the character *shō* (少, minute or very small), which is pronounced the same as the character for small, 小, but written differently.

These sizes are approximately correct, but there are minor variations within each size category.

6

Flower Patterns

SAKIWAKE (literally, "Mixed"; Irregular Stripes). Flowers that bloom in a combination of broad stripes of varying width as in the illustration are called *sakiwake*.

TOBIIRI (Streaked). This combination of irregular streaks and small stripes is called *tobiiri*, or streaked.

SARASA (Calico). This pattern of a few wide stripes and many narrow stripes is called *sarasa*, or calico.

7

SHIBORI (Tie-dyed). This pattern with a few wide stripes, many broken stripes, irregular narrow stripes, and fine dots is called *shibori,* or tie-dyed.

KANOKO (Dappled). This pattern with a few wide stripes, many broken stripes, a few narrow ones, and many, many tiny dots is called *kanoko,* or dappled.

Comment: Both modern Japanese and Western terminology for flower patterns differ considerably from Itō's. At present the Japanese use the word *sakiwake* to mean mixed flowering—that is, flowers blooming in a variety of patterns and colors on one plant. In Western azalea terminology as well, a plant of this sort is described as "mixed." The illustration that Itō provides for the *sakiwake* entry shows an azalea that the modern Japanese horticulturist would characterize as marked with vertical or irregular striping.

8

The *tobiiri* pattern is known in Japan today as "streaked tie-dyed." Itō seems to use the term to mean striated streaking that reaches all the way into the throat of the flower. Itō's *sarasa* is presently called "calico tie-dyed" in Japan, and the *shibori* pattern is known as "varied tie-dyed." *Kanoko* is called "dappled tie-dyed."

In the West, fewer specific terms for individual color patterns are in use. The term "bicolor" is used for flowers that have two concentric rings of color, such as a pale center with a dark outer ring. The Glenn Dale clone Martha Hitchcock has white flowers deeply margined with magenta and is a typical bicolor azalea. Some Japanese growers confuse the term "dappling" with "blotch"—a technical term used by both Japanese and Western azalea growers to refer to a concentration of color different from the ground color, located centrally in the upper half of the flower.

Although color charts such as the Munsell Nickerson Color Chart provide precise descriptive terms for flower colors, they are of no help in describing patterns. Because, in permuted form, Itō's terminology is still used in Japan today, it is of considerable interest to the Western azalea grower.

Flower Types

KOSHIMINO (Skirt). This structure at the base of the petals is called a skirt, and occurs with flowers of various shapes. It is drawn in an upright position to show the base clearly.

SEN'E (literally, "Thousandfold"; Double); also, SEN'YŌ. This form of flower lacks stamens, and the petals rise in layer after layer to a high point in the center.

MAN'E (literally, "Ten-thousandfold"; Anemone-flowered); also, MAN'YŌ. This form has five petals (forming a flat base) and many narrow petaloids in the center, which is low.

Comment: The *koshimino,* a curious form which gets its name from the straw rain skirt worn by farmers during the Edo period, is not cultivated to any extent today. There are still a few clones with the *koshimino,* and Creech observed it in 1982 on specimens in a collection of old Japanese azaleas being grown at the Shanghai Botanical Garden. This characteristic occurs in both the tsutsuji and satsuki groups, in particular among the clones of *R. kaempferi.* Creech noted flowers with this structure on wild plants of *R. kaempferi* in Ibaraki Prefecture in Japan. It would be interesting to look for it among populations of plants in which hose-in-hose types appear. The early Japanese distinguished it from the stand (*dan* or *dai*) and the hose-in-hose, or twofold, types. All three—the skirt, stand,

10

and hose-in-hose—are different degrees of distorted tissue arising between the calyx and the corolla. Since there are no accepted technical terms for the *dan* (*dai*) and *koshimino* structures, the translations "stand" and "skirt" are perfectly adequate. All three structures may be the same color as the flower petals or a different color. Other synonyms that Itō employs for various gradations of this structure include *kazura* (cap), *sode* (sleeve), *hakama* (trousers), and *kasane* (layers).

The flower which Itō calls *"man'e"* is usually known as "semi-double" or "anemone-flowered" in the West, and *sen'e* is known as "fully double." In both instances, the doubleness is brought about by the transformation of the stamens into petal-like structures (petaloids). Western terminology does not make distinctions between flowers with greater or lesser numbers of petals, merely noting them as having extra petals unless there is actual stamen transformation. Again, Itō uses several terms to identify gradations of these forms: *nijun* (twofold), *to'e* (tenfold), and *yae* (literally, "eightfold," or double).

VOLUME I
Tsutsuji Azaleas

General Comments

Volume One introduces the purpose of *A Brocade Pillow*, lays out the format for categorizing azaleas as either tsutsuji or satsuki by their season of bloom, and illustrates the different flower sizes, color patterns, and flower forms. It may be necessary for the reader to refer back to this Introduction until he becomes familiar with the terminology used by Itō, since we do not use the same descriptive terms for azaleas today. There is one type of flower that will be new to all readers, the *koshimino*. A *koshimino* was a straw rain skirt worn by farmers during the Edo period, and earlier. With reference to azaleas, the *koshimino* is a skirtlike structure consisting of straplike segments borne between the flower calyx and corolla. The segments may be the same color as the corolla or different. Flowers of this type are not very popular in Japan today, but Creech did see this form in a garden at Kurume. It is present in both tsutsuji and satsuki and was considered in Itō's time a delicate selection. The double forms illustrated in Itō's introductory notes are also rather interesting and rare in cultivation today.

The tsutsuji group is introduced in Volume One and, as noted earlier, includes all the azaleas except the satsuki: sixteen species, one cross, and one variety. Kirishima, the red azalea, is the standard for the tsutsuji azaleas. Its name derives from Mt. Kirishima, a peak of great religious and historic importance to the Japanese. It was here, legend had it, that the god Ninigi first descended from Heaven to rule Japan. Perhaps a potted azalea unearthed from the holy mountain seemed like a fine souvenir to pilgrims returning from a visit to Kirishima Shrine.

Identifying the Kirishima variety with a particular species is problematic. Judging from the size and shape of the flowers and the leaf shape, Kirishima most closely resembles *R. sataense*. However, that species does not occur on Mt. Kirishima, but south of the active volcano Sakurajima on a small mountain called Takatōge. *Rhododendron kaempferi*—distinctly different in habit from Kirishima—is the common azalea around the Kirishima Mountains and Sakurajima, while *R. kiusianum* is restricted to the highest elevations here and elsewhere in Kyushu. The early Japanese who roamed the Kirishima area undoubtedly combed the colonies of *R. kaempferi* for the outstanding forms, depleting the populations so that today only the poorer remnants still exist. Fortunately, *R. kaempferi* has an extremely wide distribution, occurring on all the main islands of Japan, and the more remote colonies were not similarly depleted. As a consequence, the northern populations of this azalea are far more attractive and vigorous than those from southern Kyushu. At Nikkō, *R. kaempferi* is a robust plant with a magnificent display of brick red flowers, often with dark blotches.

The first volume also contains a lengthy discussion of the Ryukyu azalea (*R. × mucronatum*), remarking that it was very commonly grown but providing no clue to its origin. The name "Ryukyu" is curious, since it really has nothing to do with those islands to the south of Kyushu. The general opinion is that it is a natural hybrid between *R. macrosepalum* and *R. ripense*. Such natural hybrids can still be seen in the wild today, especially at Mt. Aoyama near Tsu, Mie Prefecture, where *R. macrosepalum* and *R. kaempferi* grow together. Natural hybrids, between *R. kaempferi* and *R. komiyamae*, also occur, at Mt. Ashitaka, near Mt. Fuji.

Readers will be interested in the fact that the early Japanese valued azaleas that bloomed several times a year, the so-called "two-season azaleas" (Itō calls them *shiki*, or "four-season" azaleas), and several of these are described in *A Brocade Pillow*. In the United States, a clone of *R. kaempferi*, Dorsett, is an outstanding two-season azalea. Japanese growers were also aware that the hose-in-hose azaleas tended to hold their flowers long after their bloom had faded, and this was considered unsightly. We can see this same defect today, especially when the Kurume clone Snow is planted in large groups. The flowers turn an unsightly brown long before they fall off.

One azalea relative, *Enkianthus campanulatus*, or *yashio*, is included here. *Enkianthus* is a favorite plant with the Japanese because of its good garden habit and orange fall color. In addition, the bell-like flowers are appealing, especially the dark red forms. Unfortunately, we do not cultivate *Enkianthus* to any extent except in arboretum collections.

Azalea Descriptions

■ KIRISHIMA. The small flowers are deep red, surpassing all other varieties in intensity of color, and have an excellent shape. When the Kirishima azalea is grafted, the growth is poor, the plant weakens, and the flowers become paler. Plants grown from divisions or cuttings are called "pure" or "virtuous." They are of a good quality and grow to a large size, and the flowers on the old plants have an exceedingly fine color.

Comment: Kirishima is an azalea type that is said to have come from the Kirishima Mountains, but this is not certain. Although both *R. kaempferi* and *R. kiusianum* occur in the Kirishima Mountains, Kirishima may have been derived from *R. sataense* from nearby Mt. Takatōge. Kirishima is used by Itō as the standard for the flowering season of the tsutsuji azaleas. The Kirishima (also called Hiryū) azaleas are the forerunners of the modern Kurume azaleas. The Kurume azalea listed in Lee's *Azalea Book* as "Kirishima" has white flowers and is obviously not the same as the present variety.

■ Toyo Kirishima (Rich Kirishima). This is a hose-in-hose form of the Kirishima azalea with particularly good flower color. The shape is similar to the Kirishima.

Comment: Among the modern Kurume azaleas, the clone Kasane Yūyō is similar.

■ Murasaki Kirishima (Purple Kirishima). The small, very deep purple flowers are similar in shape to Kirishima, as are the leaves.

Comment: There is a present-day Miyama Kirishima azalea with the same name and appearance. The Miyama Kirishima azaleas are all selections of *R. kiusianum*.

▲ Shiro Kirishima (White Kirishima). White flowers of medium size. The petals are thick and have a sprightly appearance. The leaves are round and very pretty.

16

Comment: The size of the flowers and the shape of the leaves suggest a form of *R. sataense,* as does the fact that this variety blooms later than Kirishima. White-flowered individuals were once found in the *R. sataense* colony at Takatōge by the current park supervisor when he was a young man, but all have been removed since.

▲ Ō-Kirishima (Large Kirishima). The very large flowers have thick petals, and the leaves are similar in shape to gardenia leaves, as the illustration shows.

Comment: This is not a Kirishima azalea but a form of *R. scabrum* that is native to the Kerama and Ryukyu islands, south of Japan proper. It was brought to Kagoshima at an early date and is scattered throughout the Kagoshima area. In an herbal of 1837, *Shitsumon Honzō* (Questions About Plants), there is a print of *R. scabrum,* and among the several names listed for it is Yama tsutsuji (Mountain, or Wild, tsutsuji), so it is clear that there was some confusion about the proper name of this plant at the time. The common name in Japanese for *R. scabrum* is Kerama tsutsuji.

■ Fuji Kirishima (Wisteria Purple Kirishima). The flowers are small and deep wisteria purple. The leaves are also delicate and lovely. It blooms during the same season as the Kirishima, or sometimes a bit later.

17

Comment: This is a selection of *R. kiusianum*. Modern wisteria purple selections include the elegant Fuji Musume and Haru no Yoi.

▲ KAWARI FUJI KIRISHIMA (Fuji Kirishima Variant). Similar to Fuji Kirishima, this selection with medium-sized flowers blooms later. The leaves are also somewhat different.

Comment: This variant is probably a purple-flowered selection of *R. sataense*.

■ NIJUN KIRISHIMA (Twofold Kirishima). The flowers are the same as Kirishima but twofold; the leaves are identical. The outer segments of the flowers are shorter and paler in color. This outer layer somewhat resembles a skirt, but the segments are completely joined. Some insist that the Nijun Kirishima is inferior to Kirishima, but I find it a fine, unusual selection. Furthermore, the blooming season is longer than that of Kirishima and the flowers hold up well when used in flower arrangements.

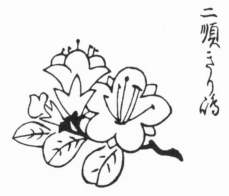

Comment: Among the modern Kurume azaleas, Minogera is similar to this variety. The leaves appear to be typical of *R. sataense*. In Western horticulture, we call this type of flower hose-in-hose.

18

▲ SAKURA KIRISHIMA (Cherry-blossom Kirishima). The pale, cherry-blossom pink color of the flowers and the smooth branches suggest a cherry tree in bloom. During its flowering season it is used in formal flower arrangements.

Comment: On the basis of color and habit this can probably be identified as a pink form of *R. sataense.*

▲ ME KIRISHIMA (Bud of Kirishima). The very large red flowers are similar to Ō-Kirishima, though their color is lighter and the leaves are smaller, with narrow tips.

Comment: In spite of its name, which identifies it as a bud selection of Kirishima, this is probably a selection of one of the many variations of *R. scabrum* that go by the name of Kerama tsutsuji. The Kerama tsutsuji resembles the Hirado race of large-flowered azaleas.

19

■ KAGOSHIMA. The flower shape is as illustrated. The color is similar to that of Kirishima, but somewhat darker. The leaves are identical to those of Kirishima.

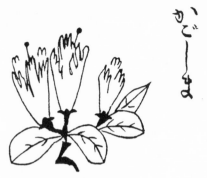

Comment: A recent clone called Kagoshima Sai may have been the same, but it no longer exists for comparison. The leaves in the illustration strongly suggest *R. sataense*. The flowers do not open fully, a peculiarity of this variety.

■ BENI KIRISHIMA (Red Kirishima). The large round flowers are a warm red with a strong purple cast, and the petals are thick.

Comment: This was not a Kirishima azalea, but was probably closest to Ō-Murasaki. It may have been a Hirado-type azalea. There is a modern azalea called Beni Kirishima, but it is a double-flowered clone of *R. indicum*, and has no relationship to this variety. Many red azaleas have a centrally located purplish blotch toward the upper half of the flower, as this variety does.

✳ YAE KIRISHIMA (Double Kirishima). The flowers are deep red and double, of the thousandfold (*sen'yō*) variety, as the illustration shows. The branches arch gracefully, like outstretched hands, and the flowers are evenly distributed over the branches, making it very suitable for the front position in flower arrangements. Although the plant resembles a tsutsuji, it flowers at the same time as Matsushima, a satsuki variety.

Comment: There are no double azaleas today of the tsutsuji type that bloom at the same time as the satsuki azaleas. This was probably a selection of *R. indicum*.

■ CHŪ-KIRISHIMA (Medium-sized Kirishima). A large light red flower.

■ OTO KIRISHIMA (Sweet Kirishima). The flowers are wisteria purple, but somewhat darker than the Fuji Kirishima. With their skirt, they have a lovely shape.

Comment: This is a selection of *R. kiusianum* with the curious skirtlike appendage, the *koshimino*. "Oto" literally means "younger brother," and, by extension, "sweet" or "cute."

21

▲ Kuchiba Kirishima (Fallen Leaves Kirishima). The flowers are a light persimmon orange color and of medium size.

Comment: Kuchiba, or "fallen leaves," refers to the russet color of the flowers of this variety, probably a selection of *R. kaempferi*.

■ Momo Kirishima (Peach Kirishima). A medium-sized peach pink flower.

Comment: This is probably a selection of *R. kiusianum*.

■ Hatsu Kirishima (Early Kirishima); also, Hatsu Murasaki (Early Purple). Small deep purple flowers.

Comment: The present-day Kurume-azalea clone Hatsu Kirishima may be the same, but it displays a blotch not mentioned here.

▲ Kochō Kirishima (Butterfly Kirishima). The very small red flowers have elongated stamens, as shown.

Comment: This is a rare flower form not seen today. The long stamens even protrude from the flower buds. It was probably a form of *R. kiusianum.*

▲ Ō-KIRI MURASAKI (Large-leaved Purple). The very large flowers are deep purple, and the plant has large leaves.

Comment: According to Bungo Miyazawa, a famous Japanese plantsman of the early twentieth century, this variety resembled the popular azalea Ō-Murasaki, except for the fact that the illustration shows five stamens instead of the proper ten.

■ KIN DAI (Gold Stand); also, NISHIKI DAN (Brocade Stand). This red flower has what looks like a skirt, but is not. Nor is it a truly double flower. This sleevelike structure is called a *dai* (alternatively, *dan*), or stand.

23

Comment: Kin Dai is probably a form of *R. kaempferi*. Creech saw this type of flower on *R. kaempferi* in the wild. One can readily see why this unique selection was named *dai*: the sleevelike segments seem to support the corolla like a stand.

■   GIN DAI (Silver Stand). The flowers are red with the skirtlike structure called a stand. Because the stand has a somewhat lighter sheen than the petals, it is described as silver. The shape of the flower differs slightly from Kin Dai, and the flower is larger.

Comment: As with Kin Dai, the stand seems to support the corolla, and is much broader in shape than a skirt. The discovery and cultivation of such a variety of selections is a sign of the skilled observation and enthusiasm of early hybridizers. Gin Dai is also a selection of *R. kaempferi*.

■ SEIZAN (Blue Mountain). The medium-sized flowers are pale persimmon orange, almost the color of fallen leaves, with red streaking.

Comment: Seizan is a selection of *R. kaempferi*. Its color indicates that it may be one of the less attractive forms of *R. kaempferi* that occur commonly in the mountains of Kyushu.

■ HITOSHIO (Once-dyed). The bright cherry-blossom pink flowers look as if they have been lightly dyed. As the illustration shows, there are five or six petals, and the flower is shaped like a lily. It blooms both in spring and autumn.

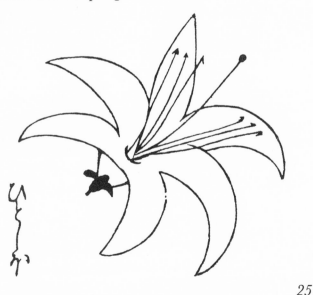

Comment: Hitoshio may correspond to the present-day Waka Sagi, a clone of either *R.* × *mucronatum* or its progenitor, *R. ripense*.

■ Yō Kihi (Yang Guifei). Beautiful, flushed cherry-blossom pink flowers of medium size.

Comment: Yang Guifei was a famous beauty of ancient China, the concubine of Emperor Xuanzong of the Tang dynasty (618–907). A Kurume-azalea clone of this description is listed in an azalea catalogue of 1909, but is no longer available.

■ Kogen Man'yō (Kogen Anemone). Red flowers.

Comment: This form is described in the Introduction. It may be a selection of *R. kaempferi*. The Kurume azalea Fukuju resembles it. There are also clones of satsuki and Hirado azaleas with the name Fukuju.

■ Yashio. The flowers, as illustrated, are roundish, resembling pepper berries, and are as white as can be. The foliage is dense, like a Japanese holly, and turns a deep vermilion red in autumn.

26

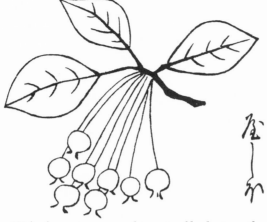

Comment: This is not an azalea at all, but rather *Enkianthus campanulatus*. It is, however, an azalea relative (*Ericaceae*) and its inclusion is indicative of the wide range of woody plants that were in vogue in Itō's time.

▲ Kōbai (Red Plum). Medium-sized deep crimson flowers.

○ Isahai (Loving Cup). Very large light red flowers.

Comment: This could be, on the basis of its size, a Hirado azalea.

■ Shimofuri Dan (Frost Stand). The flowers are red. The stand of this variety is almost white, hence the name "frost." In this

27

feature it resembles Gin Dai, but the flowers and leaves of Shimofuri Dan are very small.

Comment: The size suggests a selection of *R. kiusianum*.

▲ Ko-Zakura (Small-flowered Cherry). These light red flowers have a dark tint and are shaped like cherry blossoms.

Comment: Ko-Zakura is probably a selection of *R. kiusianum*.

▲ Shaguma (Red Bear). The flowers are red and double, as the illustration shows.

Comment: No such type exists today.

28

■ Sannō (Mountain Spirit). The medium-sized flowers are a light purple resembling wisteria purple.

Comment: Sannō is probably a selection of *R. sataense*.

▲ Ryukyu. This selection roots well from cuttings, so there is no village where this plant cannot be found. The flowers are very large and white. It is used as a root stock for grafting tsutsuji or satsuki azaleas. The graft union is good, and the quality of the plants endures. When I visited the village of Hachiōji some time ago, I walked into the mountains thinking to gather bracken fern and encountered a small straw-thatched cottage. Wondering if it was occupied, I approached and found it was a farmhouse. In front of the house, this tsutsuji was planted. Coming closer, I asked the farmer, just to see what he'd say, "Do you know the name of this plant?" The farmer stroked his beard in a wise manner and replied, "Don't you know its name? I'm sure you have it in your neck-of-the-woods. It's called the Ryukyu tsutsuji." To this I mumbled, "Oh, yes, I see." I was ashamed at having baited him, and continued vaguely, "Yes, there are all sorts of flowers in Edo, but I don't recall this particular one." And, wishing him a good harvest, I hurried home with my tail between my legs.

Comment: This is the famous *R.* × *mucronatum* that has contributed significantly to our modern large-flowered azaleas. Although it was recorded as having been introduced into the Western world as "Indica Alba" around 1819, it obviously was cultivated much earlier and was dispersed to China and various cultural centers in Southeast Asia. It has had many names both in Europe and the United States, where it was grown as "Ledifolia Alba" and distributed in southern gardens in the mid-nineteenth century. There is, of course, no wild plant of this nature, and we can only assume that it is a hybrid, possibly of *R. ripense* and *R. macrosepalum*. It is curious that it is called the "Ryukyu azalea" and unfortunate

29

that such a name could not have been applied to *R. scabrum,* which is native to the Ryukyu Islands. Instead, that species is sometimes called the "Luchu azalea" ("Luchu" being the Chinese pronunciation of "Ryukyu") in the Western world.

■ TANABATA (Festival of the Weaver Girl and the Cowherd). The small red flowers bloom in the spring and again in August. A mix of single and double flowers blooms on each plant.

Comment: The Tanabata Festival, now celebrated on the seventh of July in most parts of Japan, was celebrated one month later during the Tokugawa period. The festival commemorates the once-yearly meeting of two stars, that of the Weaver Girl (Vega) and the Cowherd Boy, her lover (Atlair). The Tanabata azalea is considered to have been a hybrid of *R. indicum* × *R. eriocarpum,* accounting for its late-flowering behavior. For those attempting to develop types that bloom twice yearly, *R. indicum* is a useful parent. On the island of Yakushima, part of the Kirishima Yaku National Park, where it is native, *R. indicum* commonly flowers in the autumn.

■ ZAI (Tassel). The flower is shaped exactly like a tassel, from which it derives its name. Grafting Zai along with other selections

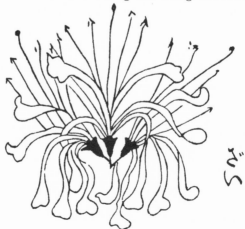

30

onto the same stock plant produces interesting results. The flowers are red.

Comment: There are several modern selections of *R. kaempferi* with straplike petals, a common one being Kin Zai.

▲ EDO ZAI (Edo Tassel). The petals of this selection, too, are split open, resembling the strands of a tassel, but the stamens stand upright. Again, the color is red.

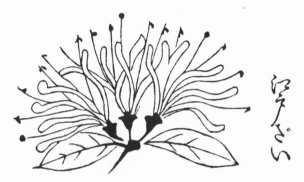

Comment: The present-day clone Sekimori Zai is similar to this selection.

VOLUME II

Tsutsuji Azaleas

General Comments

The second volume includes additional species and selections of tsutsuji azaleas. While it provides documentation of the early cultivation of several azaleas we still grow, no clues to their origins are given. Many of them were evidently cultivated long before the publication of *A Brocade Pillow*, which describes relatively advanced forms. Unfortunately, Itō did not offer any thoughts on selection methods, and it will be noted in the last section, on propagation, following Volume Five, that seed propagation passes unmentioned.

In Volume Two, we discover the enormous range of variability that exists in the species *R. kaempferi*. Although this magnificent azalea has certain drawbacks as a parent, namely, that it loses most of its foliage in winter and has an over-vigorous habit, it does produce a wide range of flower types. And, because of its wide distribution, *R. kaempferi* intergrades with several local species. The same is true of *R. macrosepalum,* a number of bizarre forms of which Itō includes in this volume. In botanical terminology, the natural hybrid between *R. macrosepalum* and *R. kaempferi* is called *R.* × *tectum.* This hybrid can be seen in quantity in the Kyoto area.

A number of *R. kiusianum* selections are described in the second volume. These have come from the Nagasaki area, where the slopes of Mt. Unzen are clothed with this species. Those listed here are the forerunners of the plants we call "Miyama Kirishima azaleas"

32

today. The nurserymen around Unzen specialize in these dwarf, small-flowered selections of *R. kiusianum,* but there are also specialists in the cultivation of Miyama Kirishima azaleas in Kurume City. The U.S. National Arboretum has a fine collection of the Miyama Kirishima azaleas, and they are now beginning to appear in nursery catalogues.

Several forms of *R. yedoense* var. *poukhanense,* a Korean species, are also described in this volume. This includes the extremely double-flowered Botan tsutsuji, or Yodogawa, and a single-flowered selection called Shiki Murasaki, which blooms both in spring and autumn. Some Japanese botanists record specimens of *R. yedoense* var. *poukhanense* on Tsushima Island, between Japan and Korea. Creech, however, did not find that species there during a collecting trip in 1978.

Rhododendron eriocarpum, or the Maruba tsutsuji, is represented by single, hose-in-hose, and double selections. This azalea also appears under the name *R. tamurae.* It grows wild on several small islands south of the mouth of Kagoshima Bay. On Yakushima, it is found around Nagata Lighthouse. It grows on coastal outcroppings on the nearby volcanic island of Kuchierabu.

The small-flowered azaleas, *R. serpyllifolium, R. tosaense,* and *R. tschonoskii,* are illustrated here but have never been used effectively in azalea breeding and remain relatively obscure. Along the rocky walls of the riverbed at Sarugajō, Kyushu, the diminutive plants of *R. serpyllifolium,* either pink or white, are remarkably picturesque. *Rhododendron tschonoskii,* the Kome tsutsuji, can be seen in many habitats throughout Japan, but the colonies on Mt. Tateyama, Toyama Prefecture, are among the finest.

Volume Two includes an illustration of *R. dilatatum* (leaves only) with the comment that it is suitable for flower arranging. There are several species closely related to this azalea (especially *R. reticulatum*) scattered throughout southern Japan. They bloom in early spring around the time of the flowering of *R. kaempferi.*

Two non-azaleas, *Menziesia ciliicalyx* and *Daphne odora,* are illustrated, probably because they are good companion plants in the landscape garden.

33

Azalea Descriptions

▲ MURASAKI TANABATA (Purple Tanabata). The flowers are light purple and the leaves are similar to those of the Ryukyu azalea. This variety occasionally blooms in August.

Comment: This is a selection of *R*. × *mucronatum* with straplike petaloid stamens. A clone of similar description was named "Fukizume Ryukyu" by T. Makino, a famous Japanese botanist, in about 1910. For an explanation of Tanabata see page 30.

■ KIN SHIDE (Golden Streamers). As the illustration shows, the crimson flower has thin stamens that resemble pine needles. Many people praise flowers of this type as elegant. The flowers are interesting because they resemble the needles of the Japanese larch (*Larix leptolepis*), especially when grafted along with other selections onto the same stock.

Comment: This is a selection of *R. kaempferi*, although the number of stamens shown in the illustration exceeds the five proper for

34

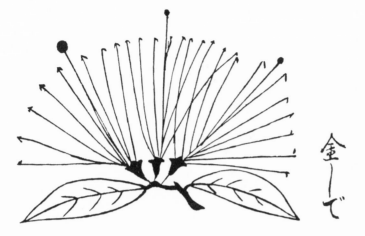

R. kaempferi. The present-day clone Kin Shibe is probably a similar selection. A *shide* is actually a paper ornament resembling a streamer presented as an offering to a Shinto shrine, but Japanese horticulturists believe that the word is used here to mean *shibe,* or stamens.

■ FUSA KIN SHIDE (Tasseled Golden Streamers). This red selection has many elongated stamens like Kin Shide and additional split, tassel-like petaloids similar to Zai.

Comment: This is a form of *R. kaempferi.*

35

▲ MOCHI TSUTSUJI (Bird-lime Azalea). This azalea has two basic color varieties, white and purple. The white variety is similar to the Ryukyu azalea and not worthy of admiration. The purple variety is light wisteria purple, and the flowers are very large. The leaves are similar to the Ryukyu azalea. The *Honzō Kōmoku* (a Chinese herbal) identifies the Yangzhizhu, or "Staggering Sheep Plant," with the Mochi tsutsuji, but that plant has yellow flowers and is poisonous. The Mochi tsutsuji described here has a sticky substance on the flowers, which is why it is called the "Bird-lime azalea." It is not poisonous.

Comment: This azalea is *R. macrosepalum,* from the Tōkai region of Honshu. It cohabits with *R. kaempferi* in many places, and natural hybrids are common. The flowers and leaves of *R. macrosepalum* are very sticky because of the glandular nature of the plant. It is unfortunate that the author did not choose to illustrate this species, because the long sepals are most conspicuous. Although the Japanese knew of *R. molle* (the Yangzhizhu, mentioned above) from the herbal literature of China, that azalea had not been introduced into Japan at this time. Its Japanese relative, *R. japonicum,* is discussed on pages 72–73.

■ SEIGAIHA (Scalloped Waves). The flowers are crimson, re-

36

sembling the star lily (himeyuri, *Lilium concolor*) in shape. The leaves are extremely slender, as the illustration shows.

Comment: The flower is rather insignificant, but the curious leaf form was highly prized in old Japan. Seigaiha is still cultivated in both Japan and the United States, although difficult to find. It is a form of *R. macrosepalum,* but the conspicuous sepals characteristic of that species do not appear in the illustration.

■ MURASAKI SEIGAI (Purple Scallops). Since it resembles the red Seigai, it is unnecessary to illustrate the flowers, which are deep purple and very large. The leaves are long, and the plant flowers in both spring and autumn.

Comment: This is another selection of *R. macrosepalum* that is no longer cultivated. Surely "red Seigai" refers to the previous entry.

▲ TAMAYA MURASAKI (Purple Gem). Very large deep purple flowers.

Comment: This is another selection of *R. macrosepalum.*

▲ DAI DAN (Large Stand). Red hose-in-hose flowers, as illustrated.

Comment: Dai Dan does not exist today, but recently a cross of a hose-in-hose Kurume azalea with a Hirado azalea produced similar types. Itō's lack of consistency in terminology, especially after his long discussion on the difference between hose-in-hose and *dan* structures (p. 23), may surprise the reader. In all fairness, the "stand" of this flower appears larger than most, and is probably the reason it is called "Large Stand." It is important not to overlook the gradual progression apparent in these special flower structures.

37

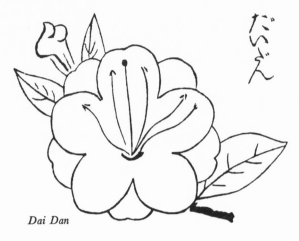

Dai Dan

▲ AMEGASHITA (The World). Very deep purple.

Comment: This peculiar type of flower, with irregular, straplike petals, still exists among the forms of *R. macrosepalum* cultivated in Japan today.

■ BIJO (Beautiful Woman); also, YAMA SEN'E (Mountain Double). The small flowers are red, and the branches of this azalea are smooth and thick in circumference. The flowers are distributed nicely over the branches, making it useful for flower arranging and especially elegant in the *suna no mono* style.

Comment: The present-day *R. kaempferi* clone Yama Sen'e fits the above description. The *suna no mono* style of flower arranging is a style in which flowers are arranged in a long, shallow, bronze vessel filled with sand.

■ KAI DAN (Twisted Stand). The small hose-in-hose flowers are light red, almost pinkish. This variety resembles Shimofuri Dan and is often confused with it. Furthermore, both varieties bloom at the same time, so the beginner is often confused and contests the difference. However, the shape of the Shimofuri Dan flower is regular while that of Kai Dan is somewhat twisted. Kai Dan is also smaller in size and darker in color.

Comment: Kai Dan is a pink hose-in-hose selection of *R. kiusianum*. The comments on the continuity between *dan* and hose-in-hose structures under the entry for Dai Dan also apply here.

■ HATSU YUKI (Early Snow). The flowers are pristine white, as the name suggests, and large. Hatsu Yuki blooms at the same time as Kirishima and is an outstanding white azalea.

Comment: This is the present-day clone Shiro Tae, which is somewhat later flowering than Kirishima. It is grown mostly in western Japan, less so in eastern Japan because it is somewhat tender. Shiro Tae was regarded by early American breeders, particularly Morrison, as an outstanding azalea. It is probably a selection of *R. × mucronatum*. Sometimes it is listed under the name "Snow Azalea," but must not be confused with the Kurume azalea Snow. Creech reintroduced Shiro Tae to American horticulture in 1961.

39

▲   MIDARE SHŌJŌ (Drunken Imp). Red flowers.

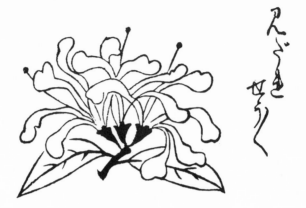

Comment: This is probably a bizarre form of *R. kaempferi*.

▲   CHŌJI (Clove). This flower does not open until after it has fallen. It resembles the medicinal clove in shape and is red in color.

Comment: Chōji was most likely a selection of *R. kaempferi*.

○   MITSUBA (Three Leaves). The flowers are purple and of medium size. As the illustration shows, three leaves are connected at one joint. From mid-autumn the leaves turn purple. Mitsuba has been used in autumn flower arrangements from ancient times.

Comment: This azalea has been called *R. dilatatum,* but it is now included by modern botanists under the designation *R. reticulatum.* It occurs in Japan from central Honshu to the Kanto Plain. It is rarely cultivated because it is difficult to propagate and not easily pruned.

■ EDO MAN'E (Edo Anemone). The large anemone-flowered blossoms are wisteria purple. The leaves resemble those of the Ryukyu azalea.

Comment: Edo Man'e is a selection of *R. × mucronatum.* The present-day clones Fuji Man'yō and Fuji Botan are similar.

▲ MURASAKI CHŌJI (Purple Clove); also, NANKIN CHŌJI (Nanjing Clove). The purple flowers are similar to Chōji, mentioned earlier.

▲ YATSUHASHI (Eight Bridges). Very large pale purple flowers.

41

Comment: This variety is very similar to Ō-Murasaki.

■ Nankin Murasaki (Purple Nanjing); also, Murasaki Ryukyu (Purple Ryukyu). Very large purple flowers.

Comment: The present-day Murasaki Ryukyu is probably the same. This is a selection of *R.* × *mucronatum*.

■ Kaisan Shibori (Tie-dyed Champion). The medium-sized flower is white with red streaks and stripes of varying width.

Comment: This was probably a striped and streaked form of *R. kaempferi*. The present-day white-flowered form of *R. kaempferi* often produces striped flowers.

▲ Mine no Matsukaze (Sighing Mountain Wind). The very large white flowers bloom in purple streaked and striped patterns. Solid white and solid purple flowers are also produced.

Comment: Similar types exist today from crosses of *R.* × *mucronatum* and *R. macrosepalum*.

▲ Tsurigane (Hanging Bells). These interesting flowers truly resemble their namesakes. As illustrated, the light purple or blue flowers are more or less arranged in two rows. The leaves are very similar to those of a holly, and identical to those of the Yashio tsutsuji.

Comment: This is a purple-flowered form of *Menziesia ciliicalyx*, distributed in the mountains and hills of Hokkaido, Honshu, and Shikoku. It flowers in June. Though rarely cultivated in the United States, it is certainly worthy of further consideration. Itō compares

the leaves of Tsurigane to those of the "Yashio tsutsuji" (*R. penta-phyllum*), a species known today by Japanese botanists as the "Akebono tsutsuji."

■ KUMOI (Sky Palace). The red hose-in-hose flowers are of medium size.

■ MISOME GURUMA (First Love). The small light red flowers have long stamens, as illustrated. This variety has a long blooming season, and the flowers turn greenish in June.

Comment: This is a clone of *R. kaempferi* now called Misome Kirishima. The use of the name "Kirishima" suggests the geographic origin of both the modern and the earlier variety.

▲ SAKURAGAWA (Cherry River). Large, fine, cherry-blossom pink flowers with light purple dappling in the throat.

Comment: This was probably a Hirado azalea that was beautifully "dappled"—blotched, in modern terminology. The Hirado azaleas are named after Hirado Island, where they were developed early in the Edo period. Creech introduced the Hirado azalea to the United States in 1961, and there is a good collection at the U.S. National Arboretum. Because of the parentage, which includes *R. scabrum* and other tender, large-flowered species from warmer parts of Japan, they will be restricted to areas from Washington, D.C. to the south.

▲ TATSUTA. The red flowers somewhat resemble a maple leaf in shape.

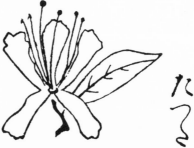

Comment: Tatsuta was probably a form of *R. kaempferi*. It is named after a place famous for its beautiful maple leaves in autumn.

■ ŌGI NAGASHI (Floating Fan). The red flowers are highly variable in shape.

44

Comment: Ōgi Nagashi is probably a form of *R. kaempferi*. This species has more variability in flower form than any species, perhaps a result of its extensive distribution, antiquity, and the degree of natural hybridization that takes place as it cohabits with various local species.

■ MINAGARA (Gazing); also, YOICHI (Night Market). The deep purple medium-sized flower, superior even to Kirishima, resembles a balloonflower.

Comment: There are natural forms of *R. kaempferi* with purple flowers. Some of these occur around the city of Hakodate, Hokkaido. Others can be seen in the southern parts of the Yatsugatake Mountains and in Shikoku. The balloonflower is, of course, *Platycodon*.

▲ KAORU (Fragrance). Large light red flowers with persimmon orange tinges.

Comment: This color is rare among the wild populations of *R. kaempferi*.

▲ GENJŌ (Pilgrim). The medium-sized light red flowers have a persimmon orange cast.

45

Comment: This variety is similar to the previous selection. Though the name is obscure, it may refer to the Buddhist pilgrim Xuanzhuang (Japanese, Genjō) who traveled from China to India and back in search of the true teachings of Buddhism.

■ Iwa Tsutsuji (Rock Azalea). Mentioned in poetry since ancient times, there are many varieties of Iwa tsutsuji. The one referred to here has red flowers like Kirishima.

Comment: Bungo Miyazawa thought the Iwa tsutsuji might be either *R. macrosepalum* or *R. dilatatum*.

✳ Awa Yuki (Light Snow); also, Yuki Zasa (Snow on Bamboo). The small white flowers have only four petals, as illustrated, and bloom in July.

Comment: This is not an azalea, but *Daphne odora*, winter daphne.

▲ Nanizo (My Goodness). The medium-sized white flowers are tinted with a faint pink haze.

▲ Usu Kaki (Light Persimmon Orange). Large light persimmon orange flowers.

Comment: The description suggests a selection of *R. kaempferi.*

■ KOI UNZEN (Dark Unzen). The lovely, small flowers are a very deep purple. The branches are thin and the leaves small, like a boxwood.

Comment: This is a selection of *R. kiusianum.* Mt. Unzen is especially interesting for studying *R. kiusianum,* as there is a great range of intermediate forms of the species to be found there. Some of the oldest nurseries that specialize in *R. kiusianum* are located around the base of Mt. Unzen, not far from Nagasaki.

▲ ASAHI UNZEN (Rising Sun Unzen). The small flowers are light red orange with a white center, and said to resemble the color of the rising sun. The leaves, too, are small.

Comment: A similar pale pink or whitish form of *R. serpyllifolium* exists today. Such types are not uncommon among specimens of this azalea growing along the stream banks of Kyushu and Shikoku. It is a petite azalea, not found in large populations.

■ USU UNZEN (Pale Unzen). The small flowers are pale purple. The shape of the flowers and leaves and the branch habit so closely resemble Koi Unzen as to be easily mistaken for that selection.

47

■ SATSUMA UNZEN. Medium-sized peach-colored flowers. Small leaves.

Comment: Satsuma Unzen, an Unzen type christened after the old name for western Kagoshima, is a selection of *R. kiusianum*.

* SHIRO UNZEN (White Unzen); also, KOGOME TSUTSUJI (Rice-grain Azalea). The white flowers are very small, as illustrated, and the leaves are smaller than a holly. This variety is used in flower arrangements, and is even regarded as suitable after the leaves have withered and fallen. Also used in *suna no mono* arrangements, Shiro Unzen blooms in June.

Comment: On the basis of the description and illustration, this must be the small alpine azalea, *R. tschonoskii*. It occurs in rocky places in the mountains throughout Japan, including the mountains of Kyushu, and is called the "Kome tsutsuji" (Rice azalea) by modern Japanese horticulturists.

■ KII NO KUNI UNZEN. The very small deep purple flowers are well shaped and delicate. Some beginners to horticulture suggest that this plant is identical to Murasaki Kirishima. It is unfortunate that they are not able to distinguish the rich, heavy feeling of the Kirishima from the more delicate, regular Kii no Kuni Unzen.

48

Comment: A selection of *R. kiusianum*. Kii no Kuni is an old name for modern Wakayama Prefecture.

○ KANOKO UNZEN (Dappled Unzen). The white flowers have light purple dappling in their throats. The branches are very thin and wirelike, and the leaves are also delicate.

Comment: This is most likely a selection of *R. serpyllifolium*. That species has a distinct blotch toward the center of the flower and is also early flowering, as is this variety.

▲ TOMOE UNZEN (Whorled Unzen); also, KOHAMA UNZEN. The flowers are light purple tinted with peach pink and have five, seven, or eight petals, as illustrated.

Comment: This was a selection of *R. kiusianum*. "Tomoe" refers to a traditional heraldic design of whorling commas, which the petals of this variety apparently resembled. Kohama is a place at the foot of Mt. Unzen. The whorled-petal form does not exist today.

▲ ZENKYŌ (Enlightenment). The small very deep purple flowers are dark in hue. The leaf and flower shapes resemble the Unzen tsutsuji.

Comment: A selection of *R. kiusianum*.

✳ KON ASAGAO (Dark Blue Morning Glory). The purple flowers resemble those of the morning glory vine in shape, and the leaves are roundish, as illustrated. Regarded as suitable for flower arrangements, it flowers at the same time as the satsuki azalea Matsushima.

Comment: This is *R. eriocarpum* (Maruba tsutsuji), an azalea important as a parent of the satsuki hybrids and the modern forcing azaleas. It occurs wild at low elevations on the islands south of Kagoshima. *Rhododendron eriocarpum* is not especially hardy, probably becuase it does not have a distinct period of dormancy, but continues to grow as long as the weather permits.

* FUJI ASAGAO (Wisteria Purple Morning Glory). This selection blooms at the same time as the satsuki azaleas. The flowers are shaped like Kon Asagao, but the leaves, though rounded, are a bit elongated. It is said to be superior for flower arranging. The large flowers are wisteria purple.

Comment: This is another selection of *R. eriocarpum,* a species which varies in leaf shape on Yakushima near Nagata Lighthouse as well as on the nearby island of Kuchierabu. The leaves of some plants on these islands are almost round and the flowers range in color from pink to purple.

* FUJI BAKAMA (Wisteria Purple Trousers). This selection, too, blooms during the same season as the satsuki. The flowers are

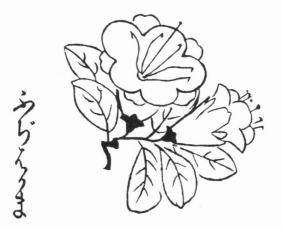

51

similar to Fuji Asagao in color, but hose-in-hose. The leaves are also similar.

Comment: Fuji Bakama is a hose-in-hose selection of *R. eriocarpum*. Its cultivation indicates that early Japanese breeders were improving *R. eriocarpum* itself as well as developing hybrids. It is interesting that Itō included *R. eriocarpum* and *R. indicum* in the volumes of tsutsuji azaleas rather than satsuki, despite the fact that they are the parents of satsuki azaleas. Undoubtedly, when Itō refers in the introduction to tsutsuji that bloom at the same time as satsuki, he is referring to the several selections of these two species which are described in the tsutsuji volumes.

✳ KAWARI ASAGAO (Morning Glory Variant). The large deep purple flowers are the same shape as those of Fuji Bakama, as are the leaves. It blooms at the same time as the satsuki azaleas.

Comment: This selection of *R. eriocrapum* is now called Datè Murasaki.

✳ SHIBORI ASAGAO (Tie-dyed Morning Glory). The large flowers are a bit lighter than wisteria purple with darker purple tie-dyed markings. They bloom with the satsuki azaleas. The flower shape is somewhat different from Asagao, but the leaves are similar.

Comment: This was a selection of *R. eriocarpum* similar to one now called Edo Nishiki.

✳ YAE ASAGAO (Double Morning Glory). The very deep purple flowers bloom in both double and hose-in-hose forms. Rarely, single flowers are produced. Against the purple background there is a darker purple streaking. This variety blooms concurrently with the satsuki azaleas.

52

Comment: A selection of *R. eriocarpum*. The present-day selection Getsu Sai is quite similar.

■ To'E Murasaki (Tenfold Purple). Medium-sized hose-in-hose purple flowers.

○ Shirasagi (Egret). Medium-sized white flowers.

Comment: Shirasagi is considered to be a white form of *R. tosaense*. This species is normally rose purple. It occurs from western Honshu through Shikoku to Kyushu. It is early flowering, as the coding indicates.

▲ Murasaki Koshimino (Skirted Purple). The very large purple flowers have the *koshimino* skirt appendages. The leaves are similar to the Ryukyu azalea.

Comment: There is a white form of *R.* × *mucronatum* with a skirt, but no such purple form exists today.

53

Murasaki Koshimino

▲ HIGO MURASAKI (Purple Higo). Medium-sized purple flowers.

▲ SHIRAHIGE (White Whiskers). Small purple flowers with white stamens.

■ HATSU SHIBORI (Early Tie-dyed); also, HARU SHIBORI (Spring Tie-dyed). Medium-sized white flowers with red streaks and stripes of varying width.

○ AKA SHIKI (Red Four Seasons). The medium-sized red flowers bloom in each of the four seasons. In the spring the plant blooms shortly after the vernal equinox, and then again in September and October. Some say that it blooms only in two seasons and is named "Four Seasons" erroneously, to which I can only reply that, though this may be true, the spring bloom continues from mid-spring to early summer and the autumn bloom continues into early winter. That is why it is properly called "Red Four Seasons." It also blooms again in winter.

Comment: This is most likely a form of *R. kaempferi*. Shiki Saki Kirishima, used especially for cut flowers because of its spring-autumn flowering habit, is probably the same azalea. In the United States, the *R. kaempferi* variety Dorsett will flower well into the winter as long as the weather permits.

○ SHIRO SHIKI (White Four Seasons). The medium-sized white flowers bloom twice.

Comment: Shiro Shiki was similar to Aka Shiki, but white. This variety does not exist today. It was probably a form of *R. kaempferi*.

▲ SEN'E SHIKI (Double Four Seasons); also, BUNGO SHIKI (Bungo Four Seasons). The medium-sized double flowers are red. It does not bloom year round unless grown in a warm location.

Comment: For those interested in fall-blooming azaleas, the fact that the early Japanese breeders not only developed this type but also extended it with color forms and doubleness should be of interest. Bungo is an old name for Oita Prefecture.

○ SHIKI MURASAKI (Purple Four Seasons); also, CHŌSEN SHIKI (Korean Four Seasons). The very large deep purple flowers bloom over the four seasons.

Comment: This is most likely a selection of the Korean azalea (wild type), *R. yedoense* var. *poukhanense*. For a more detailed discussion of its identity, see the following entry.

■ BOTAN TSUTSUJI (Tree-Peony Azalea); also, YODOGAWA (Yodo River). The very large double purple flowers bloom in clusters like a peony flower, and the leaves are large.

Comment: This is the well-known Yodogawa (*R. yedoense*), a selec-

55

tion of the Korean azalea, *R. yedoense* var. *poukhanense*. The cultivar (Yodogawa) was described prior to the wild type (Shiki Murasaki) in Western sources, resulting in the anomaly that the wild type has been named a variety of the cultivar. It should be noted, however, that both appear in this volume of *A Brocade Pillow*.

▲ Hon Dan (Main Stand). The light red, almost persimmon orange flowers have a stand resembling the hose-in-hose structure.

Comment: There is a red hose-in-hose Kurume azalea of this description today called Hōōden, but this entry suggests a selection of *R. kaempferi*.

VOLUME III
Tsutsuji Azaleas

General Comments

This volume concludes Itō's description of the tsutsuji azaleas. He continues to emphasize *R. kaempferi,* both as selections and as hybrids with *R. macrosepalum* and *R.* × *mucronatum.* Several hybrids attributed to crosses of *R. macrosepalum* with *R.* × *mucronatum* are also described. To understand the extent to which hybrids of azalea species occur in the wild, a visit to Mt. Aoyama in Mie Prefecture is highly educational. There *R. kaempferi* and *R. macrosepalum* occur in association, and many plants have leaf and flower types that are more or less intermediate. Interestingly, the selections stemming from these three species which are listed in *A Brocade Pillow* correspond in time of bloom and flower description to many of the types selected by Morrison in the development of the Glenn Dale azaleas.

Rhododendron scabrum, or the Kerama azalea, is described briefly but not illustrated. It also appeared in Volume One, but only the foliage was illustrated. *R. scabrum* derives its Japanese name from the Kerama island group, where it is native. The Kerama Islands are near Okinawa, where *R. scabrum* is also found. The Kerama azalea was introduced to Kagoshima quite early, since the Ryukyus were a stopping-off place for voyages to Southeast Asia and China. It also reached Hirado Island and is said to have been incorporated into the Hirado azaleas, a race of unusually large-flowered types. These hybrids are well represented in the U.S. National Arboretum, but their usefulness will most likely remain restricted to the southern United States where the "Southern Indicas" are grown. Except for flower size—*R. scabrum* has the largest flowers of the tsutsuji group—it is not especially useful in azalea breeding because of its lack of tolerance to cold. It is, of course, a useful parent for heat-tolerant azaleas in more tropical regions.

R. japonicum is thoroughly treated in this volume, and the Japanese were quite familiar with the different flower-color forms. The yellow phase, which occurs mostly on the barren hills of Kyushu near Seidagawa was associated with its Chinese relative, *R. molle*. The northern form of *R. japonicum*, known as Karin, is distinguished by its intensely red flowers, as compared to the Beni Renge Tsutsuji, the normal, vermillion form.

The other very important azalea in Volume Three is *R. schlippenbachii*, or Kurofune. *Rhododendron schlippenbachii* was not known to the Western world until it was collected by a Russian naval officer, Baron A. von Schlippenbach, from Korea in 1854, and not introduced into cultivation until 1893, when James Veitch sent plants from Japan to England. This was at least two hundred years after its description in *A Brocade Pillow*.

Azalea Descriptions

▲ MURASAKI MAN'E (Purple Anemone). A purple anemone-flowered variety of medium size.

▲ MURASAKI SHIBORI (Purple Tie-dyed). A very large flower with a white ground and purple streaks.

Comment: This is probably a selection of *R.* × *mucronatum*.

▲ TOKIWA MURASAKI (Everlasting Purple). Very large deep purple flowers, with leaves resembling the Ryukyu azalea.

58

Comment: A selection of *R.* × *mucronatum.*

○ FUSA DAN (Clustered Stand). This selection has red flowers in dense clusters. The branches, too, are interesting because they seem to droop under the weight of the flowers.

Comment: This is a hose-in-hose form of *R. kaempferi* which was later called the "Gera" strain. The illustration is clearly of Kaempfer's azalea and represents one of the better forms of that species.

▲ SOSHI DAN (Saintly Stand). Small red hose-in-hose flowers.

Comment: Soshi Dan is a hose-in-hose selection of *R. kaempferi.*

▲ KERAMA. Large red flowers and large leaves.

Comment: Kerama is *R. scabrum,* native to the Kerama Islands and brought to Japan proper before the sixteenth century. The

Keramas are an island group in the Ryukyus, which were a major stopping-off place on journeys to and from Japan. *Rhododendron scabrum* is scattered widely over the hills around Kagoshima City and a very old plant of this species grows in Iso Garden in Kagoshima. It has been called Yama tsutsuji (Mountain azalea) but that name is properly relegated to *R. kaempferi*.

▲ GOSHO MURASAKI (Imperial Palace Purple). Large purple flowers, with leaves similar to the Ryukyu azalea.

Comment: The existing clone Yae Yama tsutsuji is similar. Gosho Murasaki was probably a hybrid of *R. scabrum* and *R.* × *mucronatum*.

▲ NANKIN SHIBORI (Nanjing Tie-dyed). The flowers are light red with fine white stripes resembling the tie-dyed pattern.

Comment: Probably another hybrid of *R. scabrum* and *R.* × *mucronatum*.

▲ AKEBONO (Dawn). Pale off-white double flowers with a purple flush that gives a warmth to their appearance. The medium-sized flowers appear in dense clusters.

Comment: There are several azaleas today called Akebono but the one here is most likely a hybrid of *R. scabrum* and *R.* × *mucronatum*.

▲ Kō Kasan (Crimson Flower Mountain). Deep crimson double flowers between very small and small in size.

▲ Kirin (Fabulous Creature). Red flowers with laciniate petals, as illustrated.

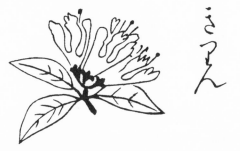

Comment: This selection does not exist today, although there is a Kurume azalea of the same name. The *kirin* was a fabulous beast of China resembling a cameleopard.

▲ Shishi (Lion). A very unusual medium-sized white flower with a wide variety of red markings, including streaks, stripes, calico, and tie-dyed and dappled patterns.

Comment: This was an extremely fancy flower, perhaps a selection of *R. kaempferi*, that included all of the types of variegation described in *A Brocade Pillow*.

▲ Tomaya (Straw-thatched Roof). A very large persimmon orange flower with purple streaks and calico markings.

61

Comment: Tomaya was probably a selection of *R. kaempferi*.

■ NATSU NO ŌGI (Summer Fan). These medium-sized white flowers are prettily shaped and display laciniate petals.

○ KO-SHIKIBU (Little Minister). Small wisteria purple flowers that are finely shaped and reach full bloom approaching the vernal equinox.

Comment: Probably a selection of *R. tosaense*.

▲ SURUGA MAN'E (Suruga Anemone). Large light purple anemone-flowered blossoms in dense clusters. The leaves are also large.

Comment: A selection of *R. × mucronatum* still in cultivation. Suruga is an old name for Shizuoka Prefecture.

■ APPARE (Glorious). Medium-sized crimson flowers.

▲ KAMO MURASAKI (Kamo Purple). Very large deep purple flowers.

Comment: The Kamo is a river in Kyoto. Dyed cloth was often rinsed in the river's current, which may be a hint to the origin of this flower's name.

▲ HANA GURUMA (Flower Cart). Purple flowers with purple-dappled throats. Large leaves.

Comment: This selection of *R. macrosepalum* still exists today, and is one of several laciniate forms, including Amagashita and Rhodoroides.

▲ KISARAGI (March); also, SARASHINA. Large white flowers and somewhat roundish leaves, resembling Shiro Kirishima.

Comment: Kisaragi is an ancient name for the second month of the lunar calendar.

▲ MAYUZUMI (Eyebrow Pencil). A medium-sized flower, a bit more red than cherry-blossom pink, with a yellowish cast.

✳ KAZANJIMA TSUTSUJI; also, NATSU TSUBAKI (Summer Camellia). This flower blossoms at the same time as the satsuki. The flowers are red dappled with purple and bloom in a mix of forms with five, six, and seven petals. This variety is often used in flower arrangements, and, with its large leaves, resembles a camellia.

63

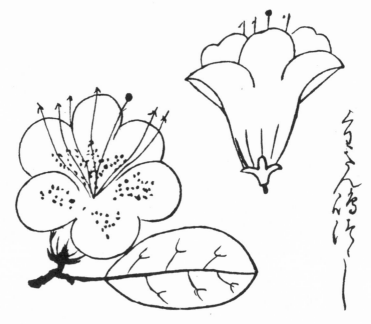

Comment: The flower color and size suggest *R. scabrum,* but the shape of the flower and regular petals are more like *R. eriocarpum.* Kazanjima is an island in the Ryukyus.

■ ŌMU (Cockatoo). Large cherry-blossom pink flowers.

Comment: The bird referred to here is probably the Moluccan cockatoo, which is pink with a deep pink or salmon crest.

▲ KUCHIBENI (Rouge). Light red in color with the margins of the petals a darker red, Kuchibeni resembles the flower of Misome Guruma. The flowers become greenish in summer and do not drop for some time.

Comment: Kuchibeni could be a selection of *R. kaempferi.*

64

Kuchibeni

▲ MIYOSHINO; also, KŌSHIN (Celestial Sign). The medium-sized flowers are white with crimson and lighter red streaks, stripes, and tie-dyed markings, blooming in a variety of patterns.

Comment: There is a Kurume azalea with this name and description in cultivation today.

▲ FUTAE MURASAKI (Double Purple). Medium-sized deep purple hose-in-hose flowers.

▲ OMOKAGE (Visage). Large white single and double flowers, as illustrated. The leaves are large.

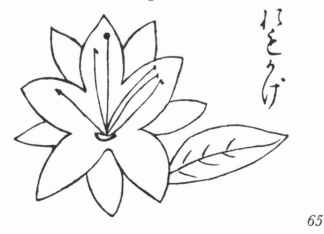

65

Comment: This selection was quite popular until shortly after the beginning of the Meiji era. It may have been a form of *R.* × *mucronatum*.

▲ O-Guruma (Little Wheel); also, Ito Guruma (Spinning Wheel); Kin Yori (Gold Twisted); Yori Kurenai (Twisted Crimson). Red flowers.

Comment: This could be a form of *R. kaempferi*. These bizarre forms with narrow, twisted, straplike petals are popular in Japan but not elsewhere.

▲ Masu Kagami (Brilliant Mirror). Medium-sized light persimmon orange flowers with red streaks.

■ Rusun (Luzon). Small purple flowers that bloom twice, in spring and autumn.

Comment: Luzon is one of the Philippine Islands.

■ Murakumo (Cloudbank). Large light purple flowers.

66

▲ Usu Kumo (Cloud Wisps). Large light-colored dappled flowers.

▲ Sekidera. Large light-colored flowers with purple streaks and a few dappled markings in the throat.

Comment: The quite variable Sekidera is a well-known azalea. It is a selection of *R.* × *mucronatum,* and was named after a famous temple in Ōtsu City, Shiga Prefecture.

■ Ogurayama. Medium-sized double red flowers.

▲ To'e Guruma (Tenfold Wheel). The flowers look like a *Clematis,* with many narrow purple petals. The leaves are similar to the Ryukyu azalea and the trunk is extravagantly twisted.

Comment: A selection of *R.* × *mucronatum.*

○ WAKA MURASAKI (Young Murasaki). Very large purple flowers.

Comment: "Young Murasaki" is a reference to a chapter by that name in *The Tale of Genji* that tells about the childhood of Murasaki, the novel's heroine. Waka Murasaki is probably *R. × mucronatum.*

■ HARU OSOHIKU (Lazy Spring Day). White flowers with red streaks, as illustrated. Unmarked white, red, and persimmon orange flowers are also produced. Some flowers have persimmon orange stripes.

Comment: The flower shape and the color combinations suggest a form of *R. eriocarpum.*

▲ TEBOTAN (Little Peony); also, FUSHIMI MURASAKI (Fushimi Purple). Medium-sized double purple flowers. The leaves are large.

Comment: A selection of *R. × mucronatum,* Tebotan is similar to *R. × mucronatum* var. *plenum,* but more double.

68

✳ Yae Ma (Double Crimson). The medium-sized deep crimson flowers bloom with the satsuki azaleas.

Comment: Yae Ma is most likely a form of *R. eriocarpum.*

▲ Karakusa (Arabesque). The red flowers of this selection bloom in dense clusters.

Comment: Probably *R. scabrum.*

▲ Kara Tsutsuji (Chinese Azalea). Very large red flowers. The flowers and leaves are similar to Ō-Kirishima but also show distinct differences. This variety is particularly well formed.

69

Comment: This is quite similar to the clone of *R. scabrum* called "Kumagai." It falls into the hybrid group called "Phoeniceum" in Lee's *Azalea Book*. Most likely both are hybrids of *R. scabrum* and *R.* × *mucronatum*.

▲ Kōji (Preacher). Large deep purple flowers.

Comment: This is one of the Hirado azaleas, a strain developed on Hirado Island and frequently employed in Japan for street and roadside plantings where large, vigorous azaleas are desired.

■ Sayohime (Goddess of Spring). Medium-sized purple flowers.

Comment: Sayohime was introduced into England before 1938 and grown by Sunningdale Nursery, Surrey, as a Kurume azalea. The description in Lee's *Azalea Book* includes petaloid sepals.

▲ Futa Emi (Double Smile). The petals look as if they are knotted together at the center. The flowers are white as snow and the leaves are large.

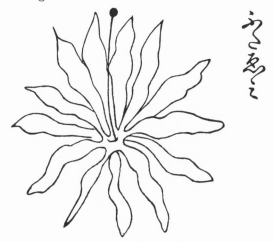

Comment: No such azalea exists today.

▲ ASAGASUMI (Morning Mist); also, GENJI MIYOSHI. Medium-sized light-colored flowers with white margins.

Comment: The white margin is unusual. Recently this characteristic has been of considerable interest when it occurs in *Camellia japonica*.

▲ BOTAN KURENAI (Tree-Peony Crimson). Medium-sized double deep crimson flowers.

Comment: There is a Kurume azalea of this description called Fukuju which could be the same.

▲ SHAMURO (Siam). White flowers with a purple calico pattern that displays a great deal of variegation, as the illustration shows. Some flowers are solid purple.

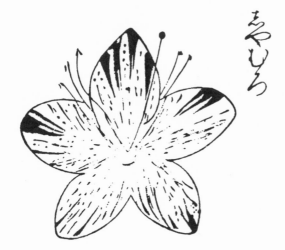

Comment: A striped variant of Ō-Murasaki. There is a present-day selection called Tsukushi Shibori that is similar. Among the Glenn Dale azaleas, crosses of *R.* × *mucronatum* and Kagetsu often produced flowers of this type.

▲ Yae Kurenai (Double Crimson). Small double crimson flowers. The flowers and leaves of this selection are similar to Yae Kirishima.

Comment: This azalea is probably a selection of *R. sataense.*

▲ Kuchiba (Fallen Leaves). Very large yellow flowers. I believe that this is the only yellow variety among the tsutsuji and satsuki. Possibly it is related to the Yangzhizhu (Staggering Sheep Plant) which is described as poisonous in *Bencao Gaomu* (an herbal printed in China in 1578). Shi Zhen, the author of the herbal, says it has few branches and grows densely, having several buds on one branch. This plant produces flowers in dense clusters, resembling a lotus. Once, on the way back from a visit to Mt. Fuji, I saw this azalea growing abundantly and in full bloom. When I asked the leader of

the group I was with the name of the flower, he said it was Ki Renge (Yellow Lotus), a very appropriate name indeed. It does not differ from the plant Shi Zhen described as growing in the mountains and valleys and ranging from one foot to five feet. The "Kalapila" flower of India seems to be the same. The leaves are as illustrated and drop in winter.

Comment: This is the yellow form of *R. japonicum*. It is common in the mountains of Kyushu, gradually disappearing as the species occurs northward. At the terminus of its distribution at Mt. Hak-kōda, Aomori, the populations are entirely red. The author is quite correct in noting its relationship to *R. molle* of China. The name "fallen leaves" may relate to the deciduous nature of the plant, but is used primarily to describe a red-tinged yellow color, or russet.

■ HANA NO EN (Flower Banquet). Persimmon orange ground with red streaks. Some flowers are a solid persimmon orange and some are solid red.

Comment: A selection of *R. kaempferi*.

73

■ YOSHINOYAMA. Very large pink flowers with white margins. When covered with flowers it looks surprisingly like an old cherry tree in full bloom.

Comment: This is a selection of *R.* × *mucronatum* related to Ō-Murasaki.

▲ KARIN (Chinese Quince). The very large flowers are deep crimson, almost coral, and bloom in dense clusters. The flower shape is similar to Kuchiba, as are the leaves, which are deciduous. This plant is also identified as the Kō Teki (Red Staggering Sheep), Eizan Kō (Eizan Red), and Tokenka (Cuckoo Flower). Although the latter is an alternative name for satsuki in general, it is glossed as "tsutsuji" in the *Gegaku Shū*. No doubt the bright coral color of the flower and the blooming season led to its inclusion in the tsutsuji group.

Comment: This is the northern form of *R. japonicum,* also called Beni Renge Tsutsuji. From about Fukushima to the northern limit of its range at Mt. Hakkōda, the flower color is crimson. The *Gegaku Shū* is an anonymous herbal of 1444. The moniker "Cuckoo Flower" was given to this azalea because it bloomed at the time in spring when cuckoos began to call.

▲ RENGE TSUTSUJI (Lotus-flowered Azalea). The very large flowers are similar in shape to Karin but lighter clay red. The leaves are similar to Kuchiba and drop in the winter.

Comment: This is the typical orange-red form of *R. japonicum.*

▲ KO-KURUMI (Little Walnut). The shape of the red flower is as illustrated. The curious flower bud looks like a shelled walnut.

74

Comment: A form of *R. kaempferi* not widely cultivated today.

▲ Koi Kō (Deep Crimson). Small very deep crimson red flowers like Kirishima. The branches are smooth and useful for placement in the foreground of flower arrangements.

Comment: This is probably a selection of *R. sataense.*

▲ Unrin (Shaded Margin). Small deep purple flowers.

■ Kurofune (Black Ship). The very large cherry-blossom pink flowers bloom in dense clusters like the true rhododendron. The large leaves are similar to the daimyo oak and arranged in a wheel, as the illustration shows. Some people use these branches for the body of flower arrangements, and they are considered very elegant for this purpose.

Comment: This is *R. schlippenbachii,* the Royal azalea from Korea. It was brought to Japan at an extremely early date and may have actually arrived from China since it is also called "Kara no tsutsuji" (Chinese azalea). It is interesting to note that while its discovery

75

in the wild by Westerners did not occur until 1854, *R. schlippenbachii* was known to the Japanese as a cultivated plant before the writing of *A Brocade Pillow*. The daimyo oak is *Quercus dentata*.

■ YAMA MAN'E (Mountain Anemone). A large red anemone-flowered variety.

Comment: Yama Man'e is a selection of *R. kaempferi*.

■ KASUGANO. Small light purple flowers.

Comment: Kasugano is probably a selection of *R. kiusianum*. It is named after a plain near the city of Nara.

76

▲ SHIUN (Purple Cloud). Medium-sized deep purple flowers.

Comment: Possibly a selection of *R. kiusianum.*

▲ SHIRO SEN'E (Double White). White flowers.

Comment: This is possibly a selection of *R. kaempferi* or a hybrid of that species and *R.* × *mucronatum.* In developing the Glenn Dale azaleas, Morrison made crosses of both of these species with Kagetsu, an extremely variable satsuki with patterns of white and purple, in an attempt to obtain very double flowers.

▲ SHIRO MAN'E (White Anemone). This is a white anemone-flowered azalea with leaves like the Ryukyu azalea.

77

Comment: This azalea may be similar to Shiro Sen'e. It is also called "Haku Botan" and still cultivated today. A clone called "Shiro Man'yō," or "Narcissiflorum," is probably the same azalea. Such azaleas are of the same origin as what we call the "Southern Indicas."

■ SUSONO MURASAKI (Purple Foothills). Small hose-in-hose purple flowers tinted faintly scarlet.

Comment: The description of Susono Murasaki suggests a hose-in-hose form of *R. kiusianum* similar to the present Miyama Kirishima selections.

■ EDO SHIRO (Edo White); also, YAMA SHIRO (Mountain White); RAKKA NO YUKI (Snow of Fallen Flowers). Very large snow white flowers with leaves somewhat like those of the Ryukyu azalea.

Comment: This is a selection of *R.* × *mucronatum*.

■ MUKASHI HATSUYUKI (Ancient First Snow). Medium-sized pure white flowers.

Comment: This is probably another selection of *R.* × *mucronatum*.

▲ KO-MURASAKI (Little Purple). Medium-sized purple flowers.

Comment: This is probably a selection of *R.* × *mucronatum*.

▲ USU IRO (Pastel); also, USU YŌ (Pale Petals). Large light purple flowers. The leaves are like the Ryukyu azalea.

Comment: This azalea is presently called Usu Yō or Murasaki Ryukyu and is said to have been developed from *R.* × *mucronatum* crossed with *R. ripense*. A planting of Usu Yō at the U. S. Plant Introduction Station, Glenn Dale, Maryland, has thrived for many years.

■ SHINONOME (Daybreak). Large warm red flowers, borne erect. When they first open, the flowers are pale; they turn deeper in color as they mature.

▲ KIKYŌ (Chinese Balloonflower). Large dark violet flowers.

Comment: This might be a selection of *R. yedoense* var. *poukhanense* because of the dark color, size, and the reference to the Chinese balloonflower (*Platycodon*) in the name.

■ ASUKAGAWA. Light purple ground with broad purple stripes. Other flowers are solid purple or light purple, and some exhibit calico and dappled patterns. The color patterns change from year to year so the variations are not fixed.

Comment: The description suggests a cross of *R. kaempferi* and
R. × *mucronatum*. This type of variegation and the ever-changing
color patterns are some of the characteristics of the Glenn Dale
azaleas.

▲ Kokonoe (Imperial Palace). Large single and double red
flowers on the same plant.

▲ Zaigyō (Western Journey). Wisteria purple flowers, as illustrated. When many flowers bloom on an old plant, it resembles
a wisteria. The leaves are large.

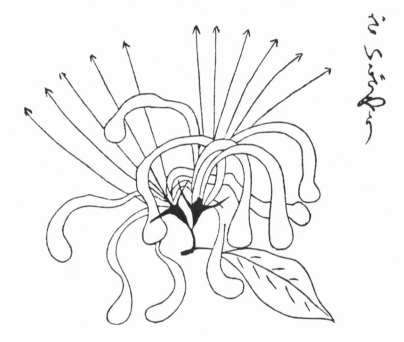

Comment: There is a clone of *R. macrosepalum* of this description
called Zaigyō in cultivation today.

▲ KAWARI KO-KURUMI (Little Walnut Variant). Large light persimmon orange flowers similar in shape to Ko-Kurumi described earlier.

Comment: Possibly a selection of *R. kaempferi* with a peculiar flower-bud form.

■ MURASAKI DAN (Purple Stand). Medium-sized hose-in-hose purple flowers.

■ MINOBU MURASAKI (Purple Minobu). Medium-sized light purple flowers.

■ KARA ITO (Chinese Thread). The red flowers are shaped like Kin Shide mentioned earlier. However, Kin Shide has long, thick stamens while those of Kara Ito are very thin.

Comment: There is a clone of a similar description in cultivation called Shibe Zaki.

VOLUME IV

Satsuki Azaleas

General Comments

Volume Four introduces the satsuki, just as Volume One introduced the tsutsuji group. "Satsuki" means "fifth month," referring of course to the lunar calendar, which was in use in Japan until 1873. The fifth month of the lunar calendar corresponds to June, and the satsuki flower about one month later than the May-flowering tsutsuji. However, since there are earlier and later selections even among satsuki, Itō has employed a coding scheme again.

The satsuki were and still are show azaleas in Japan, exhibited mostly in containers. It is the use of these azaleas as bonsai that has perpetuated many of the old cultivars until today, some plants said to be over four hundred years old. One of the best areas to observe satsuki culture is in the region around Utsunomiya City, Tochigi Prefecture.

The satsuki are characterized by heavy, evergreen foliage with oblong leaves that often turn purple in the winter. The flowers are large, thick-textured, and frequently display ruffled edges. In the most complex types, flower color varies highly on the same plant, and this leads to confusion in descriptions. Satsuki flowers may be single, hose-in-hose, or double, and the skirt structure can occur with any of these in combination. Though most satsuki are ornate pot plants, the landscape type of satsuki mentioned in the general introduction, which has yet to be fully utilized in landscaping in the United States, must not be overlooked. Some of these landscaping selections can now be found in the U.S. National Arboretum, but they do not yet have cultivar names. An excellent illustration of the use of satsuki for formal landscaping is the highway leading to the Kagoshima Airport, where densely sheared specimens of satsuki line the roadsides.

Just as the Kirishima variety is employed as the standard for the tsutsuji, Matsushima is used by Itō as the standard for the satsuki. Matsushima displays the typical satsuki diversity of patterns. Many Westerners are unhappy with the satsuki habit of producing bud sports and often attempt to stabilize them, as in the cases of white or pink Gumpo, only to find the plants eventually mixed. Morrison used the satsuki in his later Glenn Dale azaleas and encountered this problem constantly. In one case, a Glenn Dale azalea, already named and propagated, had to be withdrawn before distribution because it was simply impossible to provide a consistent color description.

The popularity of the satsuki continues unabated in Japan, where there are a very active Satsuki Society (Satsuki Kai) and several glossy magazines devoted to satsuki. Satsuki exhibitions occur around the fifth of June, at which new varieties are shown and the latest methods of pruning and styling are displayed. The plants are all, of course, in pots. Among the most famous exhibits is the one at Utsunomiya, not far from Nikkō. Foreign visitors to this show might wish to take time to visit nearby Kanuma, where the famous Kanuma soil is mined. This soft inert volcanic rock is an essential ingredient of azalea potting soil in Japan.

Azalea Descriptions

● This symbol indicates selections that bloom at the same time as Matsushima, or thirty days after Kirishima—that is, sixty days after the spring equinox.

⊕ This symbol indicates selections that bloom fourteen or fifteen days earlier than Matsushima, or at the same time as the late-blooming group of tsutsuji azaleas.

◗ This symbol indicates selections that bloom later than Matsushima.

The three symbols above are only approximate indicators, and some variation in season of bloom will be encountered.

● MATSUSHIMA. The flowers have a white ground marked with crimson and lighter red streaks, calico, and tie-dyed patterns. Several patterns may appear on one plant, including solid white, solid red, or solid light red flowers, as well as red flowers with white stripes and light red flowers with darker red stripes.

Comment: "Matsushima" refers to striped selections of satsuki azaleas in general as well as to a specific variety. Thus, Shokkō Nishiki is considered a Matsushima. Until recently, a selection called "Matsushima" existed. It was also known under the name "Variegatum." Matsushima and its related selections are highly unstable hybrids involving at least *R. eriocarpum* and *R. indicum*.

84

● TAKANE (High Peak). The shape of the flowers is similar to that of Matsushima and the color is a light red with darker red streaks. The margins of the petals are white. Solid red flowers are sometimes produced.

Comment: There is a selection today called "Mine no Yuki" that is similar. One selection with especially extensive white margins is called "Miyama no Yuki." Shinnyo no Tsuki has a white center with red margins.

● GENJI (Prince Genji). This flower has a light red ground color with red streaks and white margins. Solid red flowers are also produced.

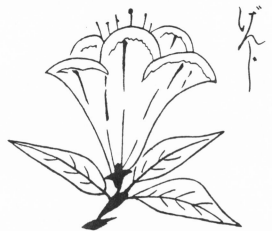

Comment: This is the present-day clone Genji Shibori.

● YOSHINOGAWA. Large, cherry-blossom pink flowers with a few red and light red streaks.

⊕ MAGAKI (Hedge). White hose-in-hose flowers with crimson

streaks, as illustrated. Both red and light red hose-in-hose flowers are also produced. If planted in a warm place, it will flower twice, in early summer and again in autumn.

Comment: This may be the present-day clone Shiki Magaki. The satsuki azaleas occasionally flower in the autumn but not to the degree that *R. kaempferi* does. This fall-blooming character may be inherited from *R. indicum,* which flowers quite readily in early winter on Yakushima, where it is native in the mountains. The upper reaches of the Issō River are a good location to observe *R. indicum.*

◑ Kōshoku (Crimson); also, Yūgiri (Evening Mist); Momi Kurenai (Crimson Silk). The small very deep crimson flowers are regular in shape and quite lovely.

● Sazanami (Ripples). Red streaks, calico, and dappled patterns on a white ground. Solid red and light red flowers are also produced on the same plant.

Comment: This is a form of Tōmei Nishiki with a white ground. It is fairly common to find two flowers, one red and the other striped or white, in the same terminal flower cluster.

◑ HAKATA SHIRO (Hakata White). The petals of this large flower are thick, and the flower is regular in shape and as white as if dusted with powder.

Comment: Hakata Shiro is especially suitable for bonsai and is in cultivation today.

● Ko-FUJI (Little Wisteria). These dark, deep crimson flowers are round in shape, as illustrated, with reflexed petals resembling the apricot blossom. It is a beautiful flower.

Comment: Ko-Fuji most closely resembles the clone of *R. indicum* Nishiki Gi (see following entry). This is a good illustration of the fact that the term satsuki covers a wide range of flower types, not just the compact, highly variable selections such as Gumpo that more closely resemble *R. eriocarpum* in habit.

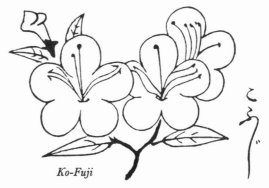

Ko-Fuji

● Nɪsнɪĸɪ Gɪ (Brocade Tree). The large flowers are white with light persimmon orange streaks and red stripes. Solid white, red, and light red flowers are also produced.

● Fᴜᴊɪ Gᴀsᴀɴᴇ (Layered Wisteria Purple). A double form of Ko-Fuji, with the same leaf and flower shape. Some of the stamens of the semidouble flowers are rather thick and protrude from the center of the flower. It is a very neatly shaped and pretty flower, the apex of the petals being round and reflexed.

Comment: The flower color, form, and leaf shape are that of *R. indicum.* Probably the present-day clones Beni Chōji and Shiryū no Mai are similar.

88

◑ Yuki Kurenai (Snowflakes on Crimson). Crimson flowers with white, flaglike appendages to the protruding stamens, resembling snowflakes. The leaves are dense, making it desirable for flower arrangements, especially in the autumn when some of the leaves turn a beautiful red.

Comment: This is a form of *R. indicum*. The red leaves in autumn and winter are particularly attractive when the plants are used in landscaping as specimens and hedges.

◑ Ko-Zarashi (Little Bleached). The crimson flowers of this selection are somewhat larger than those of the small-flowered type.

Comment: This is a selection of *R. indicum*.

● Shiogama. The large flowers have light red dappled, calico, and tie-dyed markings on a white ground. Shiogama resembles Sazanami, but the calico striping is more dense. Both solid red

89

and persimmon orange flowers are produced on the same plant, and, in addition, the leaves are marked with white stripes in the winter.

Comment: This is the present-day clone Kin Kazan. Markings on the winter foliage are common in satsuki azaleas. Sometimes they are white, but often they are wine red. Shiogama is an area near Matsushima in northern Honshu.

◖ MUSASHINO. The red flowers of this selection may have from five to seven, or eleven to twelve petals, as the illustration shows.

Comment: This is an old selection of *R. indicum* transmitted to the present day. As described in Lee's *Azalea Book,* this introduction by the Plant Introduction Section of the U.S. Department of Agriculture is white with a few flakes of spinel red.

● Ko-Kin (Small Fortune). The shape of the red flower is [long and narrow] as illustrated. The leaves, too, are long and

90

narrow, resembling the tsutsuji azalea Seigaiha. Another name for this selection is Seigai Satsuki.

Comment: Classifying this azalea as a satsuki is problematic because of the long, narrow leaves.

* ARASHIYAMA. Crimson and lighter red stripes, both broad and narrow, mark these white flowers, as well as very distinct streaks of the same colors.

91

Comment: The present-day clone of the same name differs in its description, but the modern Nishikigawa may be the same as Itō's Arashiyama.

● FUTARI SHIZUKA (Twin Beauties). Medium-sized light purple flowers with two blossoms at a single terminal, perhaps the reason it is called *futari* (twins).

Comment: This flower is named after a Noh play about a famous beauty, Shizuka Gozen.

● OSORAKU (Perhaps). White ground with crimson and lighter crimson stripes. Some claim that this flower is no different from Sazanami, but Sazanami has many calico, dappled, and tie-dyed markings, and Osoraku much more white. They are, in fact, distinct selections.

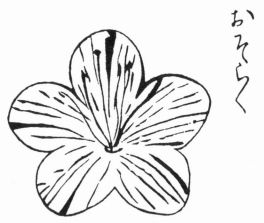

Comment: Osoraku was possibly a white-ground variant of Tōmei.

◑ SHITA KURENAI (Crimson Tongue). Very large red flowers.

92

Comment: This is possibly the present-day clone Ō-Sakazuki. The flower has a dark red blotch at the center, possibly accounting for the name. The author is usually very careful in distinguishing between red and crimson, and the discrepancy between the title and the description is one of his occasional lapses.

◑ KIRIGANE (Beaten Gold). Medium-sized deep cherry-blossom pink flowers approaching a light persimmon orange, which bloom from the end of June to the beginning of July.

Comment: Kirigane is a very late-blooming selection.

● TAKASAGO. Very large light purple flowers.

Comment: Takasago is still cultivated and used in bonsai. There is a Kurume azalea called Takasago, but it is not the same.

◑ ORIIRE (Layered Petals). As illustrated, the red flowers have five, six, seven, eight, or even up to twelve or thirteen petals. The

93

foliage is dense and dark, resembling boxwood, making Oriire superior for front positions in flower arrangements.

Comment: Oriire was similar to the present-day clone Matsunami, a form of *R. indicum*. Matsunami was introduced to the United States by Creech in 1955.

● Kōya Kurenai (Mt. Kōya Crimson). Small intensely crimson flowers. The foliage is petite and dense, and the plant has a lovely branching habit. It is often planted in combination with thick-trunked bonsai and pieces of coral in decorative arrangements because of its pretty little branches.

Comment: Kōya is a mountain in Wakayama Prefecture, famous as the headquarters of the Shingon sect of Buddhism.

● Shin Kurenai (True Crimson). Medium-sized crimson flowers.

● Hachijō Kurenai (Hachijō Crimson). Large intensely crimson flowers.

Comment: Hachijō Kurenai and similar crimson selections are forms of *R. indicum*. Hachijō is a small island in the Pacific about 120 miles south of Tokyo.

◑ Hatsure Yuki (Patches of Snow). Very large flowers of light [red] with patches of white at the margins, this selection is truly worthy of the name.

Comment: Hatsure Yuki is possibly the present-day clone Asahi-zuru, which is red with white margins.

◑ SATSUMA KURENAI (Crimson Satsuma). The petals of the very large deep crimson flowers are thick and well shaped, and the tips are heavy and pointed.

Comment: Satsuma Kurenai is still in cultivation. Satsuma is an old name for a part of Kagoshima Prefecture.

◑ Ō-MAN'E (Large Anemone); also, SATSUMA MAN'E (Satsuma Anemone). The flowers are crimson.

Comment: The uniform shape and the pointed leaves suggest *R. indicum.*

⊕ SEN'E (Double). The medium-sized crimson flowers are double.

Comment: The present-day clones Kō Man'e and Man'e are similar.

● MAN'E (Anemone). Large crimson anemone flower.

95

Comment: The *man'e* type of flower is described in the Introduction.

● Ko-Kurenai (Little Crimson). Small red flowers.

Comment: Ko-Kurenai is still in cultivation.

◑ Sokojiro (White Center). The margin of the flower is crimson and the center is white. Solid red flowers may also be produced. Underfed plants are the most highly regarded, because the weaker the plant, the whiter the centers of the flowers are. Sokojiro can be planted in sandy soil because it is a strong variety. If it is well fertilized, the branches become thick and, generally, red flowers are produced. Smaller plants produce red flowers exclusively, because the true nature of the selection dominates when young. Extremely underfed plants have very thin branches, like wires. The flowers of these fine plants are mostly white, with just a flush of red on the margins. These are called "Tsumabeni" (Red Nail Polish). The inexperienced sometimes think Sokojiro and Tsumabeni are two different varieties but they are the same.

One day on the way to the home of a person in Shiba, I stopped at a nursery in Kyobashi Street and saw two plants in pots, one labeled Sokojiro and the other Tsumabeni. Approaching, I pretended to be an inexperienced shopper and asked innocently, "Aren't these two varieties actually the same?" The proprietor came out and said, "Both the flowers and the plants are quite distinct and separate varieties. Are you sure you know anything about flowers?" In fact, it is conceivable that the truly uninitiated might think them separate flowers.

A variety called Osaka Sokojiro also exists, whose leaves resemble those of the Double Kirishima. The flower is the same as the one described here.

Comment: This variety resembles the present-day Mine no Yuki. Even today many people are confused by this flowering behavior, often attributing it to grafting different clones onto the same stock plant. There is no way to predict when these reversions will occur but Itō suggests it is nutritional.

◗ HAGOROMO (Feathered Robe). Small light red flowers, as illustrated. The leaves, too, are small.

Comment: Hagoromo is a bizarre selection of *R. indicum*.

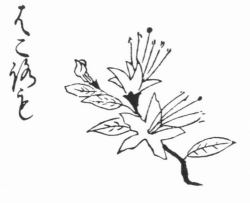

● Sнokkō (Sichuan Crimson). The flower has a white ground roughly splashed with red streaks and stripes, as illustrated. Some have light red or calico markings, and solid red, white, and light red flowers are also produced. Shokkō even surpasses Matsushima in the flower variations that appear on a single plant.

Comment: The present-day Shokkō Nishiki, one of the oldest clones with this name, is said to be four or five hundred years old. If correct, this dates the beginnings of azalea culture as early as the sixteenth century.

◑ Hiroshima Shibori (Tie-dyed Hiroshima). This is a very large white flower with a few red streaks and stripes.

◑ Meigetsu (Harvest Moon). The flowers are red and shaped like Oriire, the number of petals ranging from five to seven to eight to twelve or thirteen. The flowers are darker than Oriire and dappled [with red]. The leaves are small and dense, and the branches of this variety are often used in flower arrangements.

Comment: Meigetsu is a solid red form of Matsunami.

98

Meigetsu

● BENI SHIBORI (Tie-dyed Red). This is a medium-sized light red flower with red streaks and stripes.

◑ CHIRI (Scattered). The crimson flowers are a mixture of laciniate and normal five-petaled forms.

Comment: Chiri is similar to the present-day Sangosai.

99

◑ YUKIHIRA. Small white flowers.

Comment: Yukihira was the name of a famous poet of the Heian period.

◑ KO-MURASAKI (Little Purple). Small deep purple flowers.

⊕ YŪSŌ (Valiant). Large deep purple flowers.

⊕ KOSHI NAMI (Koshi Wave). Large crimson flowers with a structure resembling but different from a skirt. It doesn't resemble a hose-in-hose flower, either.

Comment: Koshi Nami is a red variant of Ōuchi Jishi.

◑ NANIWA SHIBORI (Naniwa Tie-dyed). Large white flowers with a few purple streaks.

Comment: This clone is still in cultivation.

100

◑ HYAKUMAN (One Million). Very large red flowers.

⊕ OIE MURASAKI (Purple Lady). Medium-sized deep purple flowers.

◑ AKARIZUKI (Moonlight). Very large red flowers with five or six petals, as illustrated.

Comment: This is a solid red form of Kin Kazan.

◑ SHIRORIZUKI (White Village Moon). White flowers with a greenish tint, similar in shape to Akarizuki.

Comment: This is the white form of Kin Kazan. It is also called "Gekkyūden." White flowers with a greenish tint exist in some clones today and it is a desirable feature.

● TOBIIRI (Streaks); also, SAKIWAKE (Mixed Bloom). Large white flowers with red streaks.

◑ KIKU MORI (Chrysanthemum Grove). The leaves of this medium-sized red flower are small and densely layered. They are even more dense during the winter months, resembling the double chrysanthemum, from which the selection derives its name "Chrysanthemum Grove." It is used in frontal positions in flower arrangements, and some also use it as the body of the arrangement. It is a very useful and elegant flower, but, because it is a satsuki, should not be given a place of honor in a flower arrangement.

◑ ŌMI (Pale Sea). The very large flowers are white with a green blotch and a few red streaks.

● KATSURAGI. Both small and medium-sized white flowers are produced, as illustrated.

Comment: This is the present-day clone Gin Sekai, a selection of *R. indicum.* Katsuragi is the name of a mountain between Kyoto and Nara.

● Asagi (Light Blue). Small white flowers with a greenish tint.

⊕ Omodaka. Very large light purple flowers with leaves as large as those of the Ryukyu azalea.

Comment: Omodaka is the Japanese name for *Sagittaria trifolia.* Perhaps the size of its leaves earned this variety its name.

● Muji Shiro (Solid White). A large solid white flower, as its name indicates.

◖ Kazaguruma (Windmill). Lovely red flowers resembling Chiri but slightly different in shape and a lighter color of red. The leaves are small, so it can be used for flower arranging.

Comment: The present-day Sangosai is similar. Kazaguruma was most likely a selection of *R. indicum.*

● Kii no Kuni. Very large red flowers.

103

Comment: Kii no Kuni is the old name of a province that corresponds to present-day Wakayama and Mie prefectures.

● Ko-Shibori (Little Tie-dyed). A medium-sized flower with red streaks.

● Hakata Kurenai (Hakata Crimson). The very large flowers of Hakata Kurenai are deep crimson in color, well shaped, and thick-petaled, resembling Satsuma Kurenai (Satsuma Crimson) very closely. The petals of Satsuma Kurenai, however, are pointed, while those of Hakata Kurenai are rounded, and Hakata Kurenai blooms earlier. There is no other [better] deep crimson flower to graft onto Kirishima.

Comment: Grafting different color forms together is one way to display them on a single plant. This method is discussed in the section on grafting in Volume Five.

● Ō-Shibori (Large Tie-dyed). The flowers are white with crimson streaks and tie-dyed patterns, resembling the tsutsuji Arashiyama, as do the leaves.

Comment: This may not have been a satsuki but rather a selection of *R. kaempferi*.

◐ Kikyō (Chinese Balloonflower). Large purple flowers similar to the Chinese balloonflower [*Platycodon*] in color.

● Mikawa Murasaki (Mikawa Purple). Large deep purple flowers.

104

◖ SEIHAKU (Green and White). Medium-sized white flowers with a greenish tint.

● NATSUYAMA (Summer Mountain). Red streaks and stripes mark the large light persimmon orange flowers. The plant also produces solid red and solid light persimmon orange flowers.

Comment: This azalea is a selection of *R. indicum,* or possibly a hybrid of *R. indicum* with *R. eriocarpum.*

⊕ SAOYAMA. Large cherry-blossom pink flowers with dappling in their throats.

Comment: Saoyama is a famous mountain in Nara Prefecture well known for its lovely display of maple leaves in autumn.

● FUTA OMOTE (Two Faces). Red and white flowers bloom on the same plant, as well as red flowers with white stripes. The stripes of this selection are always broad.

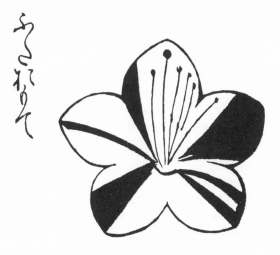

Comment: This pattern of producing two colors of flowers on the same plant, sometimes side by side, is often observed in striped selections of satsuki azaleas.

● Kochō (Butterfly). Very small red flowers with long stamens, as illustrated.

● Tsuruga Shibori (Tsuruga Tie-dyed). Very large white flowers with red and lighter red streaks. Solid red and solid lighter red flowers also bloom on the same plant.

● Satsuma Murasaki (Purple Satsuma). Very large deep purple flowers.

Comment: The present-day clone Shiō is similar.

◑ Katsuyama. This persimmon orange flower is marked with red streaks and tie-dyed patterns. The edges of the petals are rounded and prettily shaped. Solid persimmon orange flowers also bloom on the same plant.

106

Katsuyama

⊕ HANAZOROE (Galaxy of Flowers); also, KINSHŪSAN (Brocade Mountain). This selection blooms in a mix of white, red, and persimmon orange in calico, tie-dyed, and dappled patterns. Solid red, light red, and white flowers are also produced.

Comment: The shape of Hanazoroe is similar to Tōmei Nishiki, but the ground color is different.

107

◑ OMINAMESHI. The very white medium-sized flowers are similar to Oriire, the number of petals ranging from eight or nine up to, rarely, fourteen or fifteen. This is an extremely lovely flower.

Comment: The present-day clone Takachie, a solid white variant of Matsunami, is the same. Ominameshi is the Japanese name for *Patrinia scabiosaefolia*.

◑ ICHIYŌ (Petal). Small light red flowers.

⊕ FUJI SARASA (Wisteria Purple Calico); also, SARASA SHIBORI (Calico Tie-dyed). The white flowers are marked with red and light red calico, dappled, and tie-dyed patterns. Many different colors appear on one plant, including solid red, white, and light red flowers.

● SHIRANAMI (White Wave). The large white flowers appear to be lightly tinted with cherry-blossom pink and exhibit a few red streaks.

◑ ZAI (Tassel). The contorted petals of these red flowers are, as illustrated, shorter and more twisted than those of the Zai Tsutsuji.

Comment: This is probably the present-day Kin Zai, a fine plant for bonsai. Creech introduced Kin Zai to the United States in 1955.

◑ UKIGUMO (Drifting Clouds). The very light [red] large flowers are well formed and delicate. Dappled markings can be found in the flowers' throats.

◑ SHIMO MURASAKI (Purple Frost). Very large light purple flowers.

● NERI KINU (Glossy Silk). Large white flowers with a cherry-blossom pink blush.

● AZANASHI (Immaculate). Large light red flowers.

● HIGURASHI (Sunset). Large cherry-blossom pink flowers with such fine dots that it is difficult to tell whether they are dots or dappling.

109

● UTSUSEMI (Cicada Shell). These large persimmon orange flowers bloom marked with various combinations of red calico and tie-dyed patterns and white streaks.

● SATSUMA SEN'E (Satsuma Double). Double crimson flowers.

Comment: Probably a selection of *R. indicum.*

◑ TOYO SATSUMA (Rich Satsuma). Large very deep crimson hose-in-hose flowers.

◑ MIIDERA. The large white flowers are marked with purple and light purple streaks and calico patterns. Solid light purple and white flowers also bloom on the same plant.

⊕ HANA KAGAMI (Perfection). The light persimmon orange flowers are marked with red stripes, calico, and dappled patterns. Light red flowers also appear on the same plant.

110

Hana Kagami

● KIYO TAKI (Clear Waterfall). The white flowers are marked with red stripes of varying width and light red streaks. Solid white, red, and light red flowers also are borne on the same plant.

⊕ GENJI MAGAKI (Genji Hedge). This is a hose-in-hose light red flower with red streaks. Solid red flowers are also produced, and the plant blooms again in autumn. As the illustration shows, the petals have white margins.

● Jūrin (Ten Flowers). The large white flowers are marked with red and light red calico patterns and much dappling. Solid red, light red, and white flowers are also seen on the same plant.

⊕ Shirafuji (Wisteria White). The medium-sized flowers are very white. The flowers of other azalea varieties wither on the plant, with rather unattractive results. Shira Fuji is superior because the flowers fall before they begin to fade. In addition, the flowers are long-lived, unlike those of the *gojika,* which fall rather quickly.

Comment: *Gojika* is the four-o'clock (*Mirabilis jalapa*).

◑ Murasaki Kazaguruma (Purple Windmill). Purple flowers.

VOLUME V
Satsuki Azaleas

General Comments

Volume Five concludes the descriptions of the satsuki with some of the most bizarre types. A great many of them have the skirt structure mentioned earlier. The large number of selections with this character in combination with other forms is evidence for the great popularity of the skirt in Itō's time. In the description of one satsuki, Hanagasa, the straplike flower petals are recommended as a garnish for fish salad (*namasu*) and vegetable dishes. This is likely to be the only culinary use of azaleas on record.

Itō couldn't resist listing those tsutsuji and satsuki that were traditionally the most highly rated and giving his own opinion on newer varieties, which is perhaps most significant as a clue to the varieties that had been grown in earlier times and those which were recent developments. Itō has included some of the bicolored flowers—with dark centers and white edges, white centers and dark edges, and one with a thin white rim—in this list, many of which can be found in the modern Glenn Dale azaleas. One is almost led to speculate whether Morrison, having developed over four hundred Glenn Dale azalea varieties, might not have been a reincarnation of one of the early Japanese azalea breeders.

A survey of cultural practices completes the volume, beginning with grafting methods. Itō makes a number of interesting observations about the effects of grafting, which was the conventional method of propagating azaleas. The Japanese, it must be remembered, enjoyed viewing plants with several kinds of flowers

113

on a single plant, an effect that could be achieved by grafting. Itō, however, cautioned his readers to select only varieties that bloomed simultaneously when creating such combinations, to avoid unsightly results. The approach graft, described on page 00, is still used for this purpose in Japan.

The section on cuttings offers some suggestions that will interest the reader who wishes to try something "new." One is the application of a layer of sphagnum moss in the rooting medium. (Sieved sphagnum would probably work best.) Sphagnum is highly sterile and contributes to maintaining a good moisture level for the cuttings. It may even have some value in limiting the growth of disease organisims in the rooting medium. Itō recommended setting the cuttings directly into open beds in the ground. In Japan, and also in China, woody cuttings are still set directly into ground beds in the early spring. While visiting a tea research station in Huangzhou, China, I saw thousands of cuttings of commercial tea rooted in shaded beds in this manner.

Itō makes some interesting comments on manures, but the decision to follow these recommendations can only be left to the better judgment of the individual reader. Nevertheless, the suggestions on the use of old leaves are just as good now as they were in Itō's time.

Azalea Descriptions

● SODE MAGAKI (Sleeve Hedge). The flowers are white with red streaks and dapples, and are, as the illustration shows, hose-in-hose. The branches are slender, and many flowers bloom in clusters, so that the plant recalls a weeping cherry. This is a rare selection produced in recent years.

Comment: The present-day clone Futae Zuru is similar. Itō's remark that this is a recent rare selection indicates that there must have been considerable activity among breeders at the time. Sode Magaki exhibits an especially fine flower type, as the petaloid

114

sleeve also bears the variegations. Here Itō introduces another synonym for hose-in-hose: sleeve (*sode*).

● SODE KANOKO (Dappled Sleeve). The flower shape appears to be very similar to Sode Magaki, but there are many more dappled markings. Red and light red flowers are also produced, and the plant occasionally blooms in September.

Comment: This is a ground-color variant of Futae Zuru.

● HANA GATAMI (Flower Keepsake). The white flowers are regular in shape with pointed petals, and bloom in variable red,

light red, and persimmon orange patterns of tie-dyed and calico markings. The plant also produces solid white, red, and light red flowers.

Comment: The present-day clone Sankō is similar. These highly variable types are difficult to maintain. Morrison once discarded a Glenn Dale selection after it was named but before release because it was so variable that he could not provide a constant description.

● YASHIRO (Eight White). The large, solid white flowers are shaped like Matsushima. This is a truly superior white selection.

Comment: A white-ground selection of Shokkō Nishiki.

◑ KAGURAOKA. The flowers are white with deep crimson calico markings, light red with tie-dyed markings, or red with white or light red streaks. All of these types bloom on the same plant in addition to a variety of calico and dappled patterns. This is a recently developed rarity.

116

Comment: The present-day clone Kaguraoka is the same.

● SHARE MOKU (Dandy Tree). The light persimmon orange flowers are of a very stylish shade. The very large flowers are finely shaped and thick-petaled. A few red streaks mark the petals.

Comment: With no illustration and so general a description, it is not possible to equate this selection with a present-day clone.

⊕ NISHIKI (Brocade). The deep crimson flowers are hose-in-hose. Though a satsuki in habit, it blooms earlier than Kirishima and again in October and November, producing more flowers than other year-round blooming azaleas. Because of its satsuki habit, the branches and leaves are dense. This, in addition to the fact that it blooms twice, in seasons when flowers are scarce, makes it a much-prized flower for flower arrangements.

Comment: This is a solid color form of Nishiki Gasane.

● TOSSŌ MURASAKI (Purple Cockscomb). Large purple flowers.

117

● Mumegae (Plum Branch). The small red flowers are very prettily shaped and borne in both hose-in-hose and double forms.

● Genji Shibori (Genji Tie-dyed). This is similar to the Genji mentioned earlier, with many tie-dyed markings.

Comment: Presently in cultivation.

◑ Oku Murasaki (Late Purple). This variety has large very deep purple flowers and dark-colored leaves, making it useful for flower arrangements.

Comment: This is probably the present-day Shiō.

● Uranami (Surf). The red flowers are marked with white calico and streaked patterns. Solid red and solid white flowers are also produced, and all flowers have a skirt. Since most flowers are white with red markings, this red flower with white striping is much admired by many.

Comment: The present-day clone Kurui Jishi is similar. Note that this flower has the typical skirt segments, though their color is not described.

118

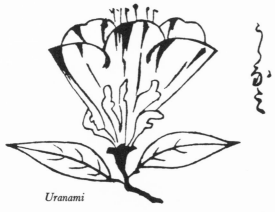

Uranami

◑ OTOWA TAKANE (Otowa Peak). The very large flowers are light red with red streaks. Solid red and light red flowers are also produced.

⊕ BENI MAGAKI (Red Hedge). Crimson flowers.

Comment: This fine hose-in-hose crimson satsuki is still in cultivation.

119

◖ KASHIWAZAKI. The white flowers are marked with purple streaks. Solid purple and white flowers are also produced. The medium-sized flowers are very well shaped. The leaves are small and pretty and the foliage dense, making it useful in flower arranging.

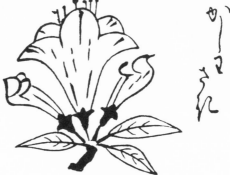

◖ CHŌYŌ (Chrysanthemum Festival). The very large white flowers are marked with clear-cut crimson streaks.

⊕ SEKIMORI (Barrier Guard). The crimson flowers resemble Kirishima, and both single and double blossoms are produced.

Comment: This is one of the early-flowering satsuki that could have a tsutsuji parent.

◑ KO-TSUBAKI (Little Camellia). The flowers are a bit more purple than pink, and bloom, as illustrated, in hose-in-hose and three-layered (double hose-in-hose) forms, as well as single flowers from which petaloid stamens protrude. It also produces anemone-flowered types.

Comment: This azalea is still in cultivation as Warai Jishi. It was used occasionally by Morrison in crosses with Vittata Fortunei, and the Glenn Dale azaleas from this combination are also double or semidouble. The hose-in-hose type is not cultivated in the United States.

● Ō-FUJI (Large Wisteria Purple). Very large crimson flowers.

Comment: Direct crosses of *R. eriocarpum* and *R. indicum* produce such flowers. It is interesting to note the discrepancy between the name and Itō's color description.

121

◖ RAKAN (Buddha's Disciple). Large deep purple flowers. The leaves are dark-colored and dense. The lovely branch habit of Rakan make it excellent for frontal placement in flower arrangements, especially in winter.

● OSAYA (Sheath). Very large deep crimson flowers.

● HANA KAZURA (Flowered Cap). Red streaks mark the white flowers, which have a skirtlike structure resembling a *koshimino*.

Comment: This is an exceptionally neat flower form worthy of consideration by breeders today. There has been a debate, recently, as to exactly where the hose-in-hose tissue arises. Generally, it has been considered to be a distortion of the calyx, but others have observed that it originates from the base of the corolla. Itō's illustration would suggest the latter view is correct. Furthermore, the fact that the color of the hose-in-hose structure is similar to the petals suggests that origin, rather than the calyx.

◖ HANAGASA (Flower Parasol). Very deep crimson, these flowers are sometimes sprinkled on fish or vinegared salad dishes, the narrow petals making an elegant garnish for these dishes.

Comment: An old clone, Mai Shōjō, is similar, but it is rare. This is probably the only reference to the use of azalea flowers as a garnish.

● BENI MURASAKI (Magenta). The medium-sized purple flowers have a warm, reddish tint.

● HITOMARU. The flower texture is thick and firm, and the flowers are a warm shade of persimmon orange with red and white stripes. The blossoms of this rare type developed in recent years are large and showy.

Comment: Still in cultivation today and very desirable for bonsai, Hitomaru is named after a poet of the seventh century.

123

◑ TATSUNAMI (High Wave). This variety produces white flowers marked with red stripes and persimmon orange streaks, and orange flowers marked with red streaks and calico patterns. Both types of flowers bloom on the same plant and are very prettily formed.

Comment: A highly variable satsuki. A similar selection was introduced from Japan by Creech in 1955.

● TAMA KAZURA (Jeweled Cap). The flowers are light persimmon orange with red streaks and a caplike structure at the base of the petals.

124

Comment: This is one of the unusual flower types with a petaloid cap between the calyx and corolla. It is not exactly a hose-in-hose, but approaches it in structure.

● Fuji Takane (Fuji Peak). The large flowers are slightly deeper than light [red], with red—almost persimmon orange—streaks. Solid red and light red flowers are also produced.

● Moku Shibori (Wood-grain Tie-dyed). The very large flowers seem at first to be cherry-blossom pink, but have a warm, yellowish hue that is even prettier and suggests the color of the tree peony Mo'an. Red streaks mark the blossoms.

● Ito Kurenai (Crimson Strands); also, Chūyō (Moderation); Yae Shide (Double Streamers). Red flowers.

Comment: It is surprising that so distinct a form is described so simply, but probably the illustration suffices to identify it.

125

● TAKAMATSU (Tall Pine). The persimmon orange blossoms are marked with red stripes, broken stripes, and dapples. Solid red flowers are also produced.

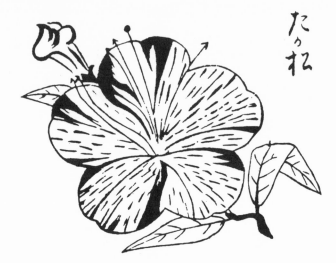

Comment: The present-day clone Kin Nishiki is similar. There is a clone called Takamatsu, but the ground color differs.

⊕ OSHIO (Tide). The large light red flowers are marked with red stripes of varying width. Solid red and light red flowers are also produced.

● SEIJI (Porcelain). Large cherry-blossom pink flowers.

Comment: The present-day clone Gosho Zakura, which was introduced by Morrison in 1938, is similar.

○ MINE NO YUKI (Snow on the Peak). The center of the flower is pale pink and the outer margin bright white. The flowers are well shaped and very rich in appearance. Some have red streaks. This selection is one of the rare new varieties of recent years.

Comment: This exceptionally fine bicolor is still cultivated. The flowers are very large and thick in texture.

● Usu Yuki (Light Snow). The petals of this superior very large white flower are thick, and the flowers are regular in shape.

◗ Daruma Murasaki (Daruma Purple). Very large deep purple flowers.

● Hana no Moto (Outstanding Flower). The white flowers are marked with red streaks and orange and light red calico markings. Hana no Moto blooms in a wonderful combination of patterned and solid white, red, and light red flowers that defies description and differs from branch to branch. In the winter, the leaves are

127

marked with purplish streaks. Since the foliage is quite dense, it is often used for frontal positions in flower arrangements. This is one of the rare recent varieties.

Comment: Still cultivated as Kin Kazan. This clone again illustrates the superb quality of azaleas of the early Edo period. We see this type of flower among the Glenn Dale azaleas. The purple mottling of the foliage in winter is a special characteristic of the satsuki azalea. It occurs on the leaves of seedlings of crosses between *R. eriocarpum* and *R. indicum*.

● NATSU KIRISHIMA (Summer-blooming Kirishima). The color of these large deep crimson flowers is so fine that they have earned the name Kirishima. The foliage is dense and regarded as without compare for flower arrangements. The foliage becomes even more dense in fall and winter.

⊕ KASHŪRON (Name obscure). This is a hose-in-hose persimmon orange flower with red streaks. Solid [orange] flowers are also produced, and the plant blooms in both summer and autumn.

128

Comment: This selection is in cultivation today as Kokonoe Nishiki.

⊕ MAKI GINU (Silk Roll); also, KIRITSUBO (Paulownia Court). Red flowers.

Comment: This name appears in *Kadan Kōmoku* (1664) and is also discussed in a Japanese satsuki catalog of 1909, though the description differs slightly. This was certainly one of the most double flower forms judging by the illustration, and it is odd that this feature is not mentioned by Itō.

129

● BENI BOTAN (Red Tree Peony). Red flowers.

● FUJI NAMI (Wisteria Purple Wave). The white flowers bloom in various combinations of red and light red calico and streaked patterns.

130

● Momiji Kasane (Layered Maple). Red flowers.

Comment: *Kasane,* meaning layered, is another Japanese term to describe the hose-in-hose flower and is synonymous with *futae* (translated as hose-in-hose). In addition, we have encountered the use of the terms skirt, stand, and cap, which are perhaps less developed forms of the hose-in-hose structure. The terms *yae,* *sen'e,* and *man'e,* which have appeared in several entries, refer to double flowers brought about by transformation of the stamens or simple increase in petal number, and again are degrees of modification. It is possible to have combinations of both types of "double" flowers.

● Ichimonji (Number One). The red flowers have white stripes. Solid red and solid white flowers are also produced, as are white flowers with red streaks.

● Onjōji. The very large flowers are a light orangish color with red streaks and light purple stripes.

Comment: Onjōji is a temple in Ōtsu, Shiga Prefecture.

131

⊕ KINUGAWA. The very large flowers are a warm cherry-blossom pink color streaked with red.

● MURASAME (Shower). The white flowers are marked, as illustrated, with red and light red calico, dappled, and tie-dyed patterns. Solid red and light red blossoms are also produced, all types blooming in a variety of combinations.

● AZUMA KURENAI (Crimson East). Very large red flowers.

● YOSHINO MURASAKI (Purple Yoshino). Very large purple flowers.

● OTOWAYAMA. The white flowers are marked with deep red tie-dyed markings. Some flowers are light red with red streaks. The mix of white, red, and light red flowers is very pretty. Occasionally six-petaled flowers bloom. They are larger in size than Matsushima.

132

Comment: The present-day clone Sankō Nishiki is similar. Sankō no Tsuki may also be a variant, for it has six petals.

● ONOE. The white flowers are marked with red or light red calico, dappled, and streaked patterns as illustrated.

Comment: The present-day clone Nishikigawa is probably similar.

133

● GEMPEI (Red and White). As illustrated, the upper part of the flower is red and the lower part is white.

Comment: The petaloid tissue here is less developed than in a hose-in-hose selection, but is rather interesting because the "cap" is white. (The differently colored layers are labeled in the illustration.) The name refers to the heraldic colors of the two feudal clans, the Minamoto (Gen) and the Taira (Hei, or Pei), whose clashes date back to the twelfth century.

● SEIYŌ (Western World). Very large cherry-blossom pink flowers with a skirt.

◑ GENJI MURASAKI (Purple Genji). The small purple flowers are edged in white. With its small leaves, it is suitable for front positions in flower arrangements.

◑ OSAKA HANAGURUMA (Osaka Flower Cart); also, ROKKEN (Name obscure). The red flowers have five or six petals.

Comment: This is most likely a selection of *R. indicum*.

134

Osaka Hanaguruma

● MATSUNAMI (Pine Wave). The white flowers bloom in a bold pattern of red and light red calico and dappled markings. Solid white, red, and light red flowers are also produced.

Comment: This selection still exists and there are several similar variants such as Chiyoda Nishiki and Meigetsu. Creech introduced

135

both Matsunami and Chiyoda Nishiki into the United States in 1955.

● Usu Kasane (Pale Layers). Light red.

Comment: This hose-in-hose variety is probably a selection of *R. indicum.*

● Matsushima Koshimino (Skirted Matsushima). This is similar to Matsushima, with the addition of a skirt.

● Busō Koshimino (Skirted Exemplar). The large persimmon orange flowers are marked with red streaked, calico, and dappled patterns, and bloom in combination with solid red and persimmon orange flowers. There is a skirt.

Comment: The two entries above are fine examples of the selection of variants with the skirt. We cannot expect to find this type today since the skirt evidently lost its popularity in Japan early in the twentieth century, and in the Western world is not even known.

136

● GENJI KOSHIMINO (Skirted Genji). The pale [red] flowers are marked with red streaks and have white margins.

Comment: Probably a white-margined Kurui Jishi. This selection must have been exquisite with its white rim and the many-segmented skirt.

● SHIRO KOSHIMINO (Skirted White). Although this variety is called white, it has a few red streaks. The large flowers have a skirt.

● KAKI KOSHIMINO (Skirted Persimmon Orange). The large persimmon orange flowers have a skirt and are marked with red streaks. Solid red flowers are also produced.

● OSORAKU KOSHIMINO (Skirted Perhaps). The flowers have a white ground marked with red and light red stripes. A combination of white, red, and orange flowers are also produced. There is a skirt.

Comment: The present-day selection Kurui Jishi may be the same.

137

Osoraku Koshimino

● AKA KOSHIMINO (Skirted Red). This flower has a structure resembling but distinct from a skirt. The shape is only slightly similar but since it has been known by the name "Skirted" for so long, it will hardly do to change it now. This variety blooms in a fashion similar to Kazaguruma.

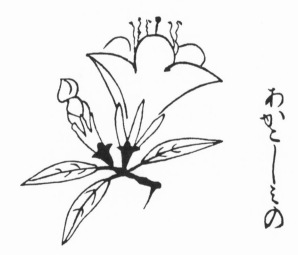

● SAZANAMI KOSHIMINO (Skirted Ripples). This is like the Sazanami mentioned earlier, but with a skirt. The flower shape and color patterns are otherwise identical.

Comment: Sazanami Koshimino and Aka Koshimino are the same color, differing only in the degree of development of the skirt. Shiroji Tōmei is similar but lacks the skirt entirely.

◑ KAPPA KOSHIMINO (Skirted Cape). Although it is called "skirted," this variety is actually more of a hose-in-hose flower, as the skirt is especially well formed, so perhaps "cape" is a better term to describe it. The flowers are red.

Comment: "Kappa" comes from the Portuguese for "cape." The original object of clothing resembled a poncho, making it entirely appropriate for describing this petal structure.

● Ō-KOSHIMINO (Large Skirted). The very large red flowers have a skirt.

● TAKANE KOSHIMINO (Skirted High Peak). Similar to Takane, described earlier, but with a skirt.

Comment: Probably Mine no Yuki with a skirt. This is a bicolored type with a red center and white margin.

● YAE KOSHIMINO (Skirted Double). A fine double red flower with a well-formed skirt.

Comment: Probably the present-day clone Shishi Botan, this variety offers an instance where the skirt is combined with the increase in petals (*yae*) known as doubleness.

● AZANASHI KOSHIMINO (Skirted Immaculate). Large red flowers with a skirt.

140

Favorite Selections and
Notes on Culture

Five Tsutsuji Azaleas

KIRISHIMA (crimson)
RYUKYU (white)
IWA TSUTSUJI (red)
SHIRO SEN'E (white, double)
KUROFUNE (cherry-blossom pink)

These five azaleas have been famous as "the five tsutsuji" from olden times. As mentioned earlier, Ryukyu and Iwa tsutsuji are not especially fine selections, but they have been admired since ancient times and so are still often praised.

Comment: This is an interesting list because it includes Kurofune (*R. schlippenbachii*), an introduced azalea from Korea. The fact that these azaleas were "admired since ancient times" indicates that the interest in azaleas may go back several generations prior to the Edo period.

Three Satsuki Azaleas

MATSUSHIMA (variegated flower)
GENJI (light red)
SATSUMA KURENAI (crimson)

These varieties are known as "the three satsuki" and have been much admired from times of old. In fact, it is because of their antiquity that they are so highly praised. In recent years, five truly marvelous and superior-shaped flowers have been developed that have displaced them:

MINE NO YUKI (pink and white)
HITOMARU (persimmon orange with white stripes)
KAGURAOKA (variegated flower)
KO-TSUBAKI (purple hose-in-hose)
HAKATA HAKU (white)

These five selections have well-shaped and superior flowers. Together with the first three, they are known as "the eight satsuki."

Grafting

The best time for grafting is from the month of March until the middle of June. Saw off the trunk of the stock and shave away any trace of the saw cut. Then scrape off the bark near the cut until none remains. It is a mistake to scrape deeper than the outer bark layer. Do this to both the stock and the scion. The length of the scraped area should be about 1.8 to 2.1 centimeters. It is especially important that the knife should be well sharpened. A knife that has been used to cut something salty or alkaline is extremely harmful. Grafting is much more successful with a knife that cuts well. No matter how skilled you are, remember: it is a living tree that is being cut, and rough handling will be fatal. In fastening the twine, do not tie it too loosely or too tightly. If it is too tight, the bark will peel off, and if it is too loose, the graft will not unite. It should be tied only tight enough to prevent the scion from moving. Twine made from raw hemp fiber soaked in hot water is fine, but untreated raw hemp is harmful.

As the illustration shows, wrap the union with a fallen bamboo sheath, being careful not to let water accumulate at the graft site

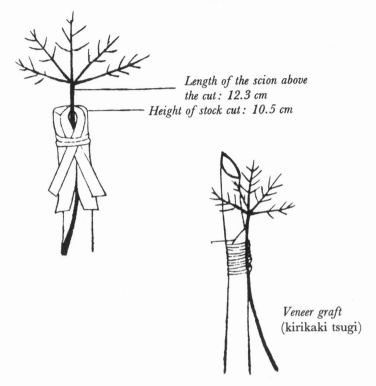

Length of the scion above the cut: 12.3 cm
Height of stock cut: 10.5 cm

Veneer graft
(kirikaki tsugi)

during the rainy season. If there is excess water, the graft site will be damaged and the twine will decay. The graft will also suffer if exposed to direct sunlight.

Grafting may also be done from mid-June to early August. This is called "*doyō*," (a Chinese calendrical term for summer) grafting. At this time, it is not desirable to cut back the stock, because the cut will be exposed to strong sun and the plant will be weakened. It is also bad to try to graft without making any cut. Rather, a cut should be made into the trunk as illustrated—1.2 to 1.5 centimeters is the ideal length—and a veneer graft (*kirikaki tsugi*) made. The top of the trunk can then be cut off the following spring. Do not remove the top too soon, or the graft will be injured by wet and cold; in the spring, around the equinox, is the best time. Wrap the graft with a bamboo sheaf.

Grafting by the Separate Graft Method (*Tsugiwake*)

Many grafts can be made on a large stock plant. This is called vertical grafting, or *rikka tsugi*.

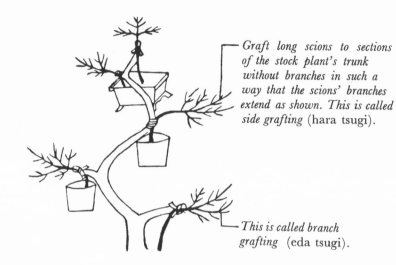

Graft long scions to sections of the stock plant's trunk without branches in such a way that the scions' branches extend as shown. This is called side grafting (hara tsugi).

This is called branch grafting (eda tsugi).

When making a graft toward the top of a plant, plant the scion in a light wooden container and hang it from the branch with a wire or a bracken rope. Water frequently, and be sure to provide drainage holes in the bottom. In September, open the bamboo sheath, cut off the bottom of the scion, and cover again with a bamboo sheath. It is all right to transplant the stock at this time, but it is bad to transplant too often. You may think you are being kind to your beloved azaleas, but the Chinese plantsman [Guo] Tuotuo has stated that it is harmful to transplant too frequently, and he is correct.

Comment: Guo Tuotuo, or "Camel-back Guo," was a plantsman of ancient China. He was named Camel-back because of his humped back, and the name came into use as a general term for gardeners after Guo's story was popularized by the Tang-dynasty literatus Liu Zongyuan in his *Biography of the Gardener Guo Tuotuo*.

There is little to add to Itō's remarks on grafting, especially since the practice has largely been replaced by the highly successful method of propagation by cuttings. Grafting was, of course, in vogue prior to the twentieth century. The observations concerning the need for protecting the graft union against the elements remain perfectly accurate with respect to the grafting of other woody plants, with which cuttings are not so successful as they are with azaleas. Perhaps the only instance in which grafting would be used in azalea propagation today is when a selection is extremely weak and it is difficult to obtain cuttings. In that case, grafting can be employed in the manner that Itō describes as branch grafting. Nowadays the end of the scion would be placed in a small plastic container, as is so often done with camellias.

Cuttings

Build a flower bed by setting up a boxlike frame six centimeters in height and filling it evenly with finely sifted black soil to a depth of three centimeters. Spread a 1.5 centimeter layer of sand over this. It is especially important to screen out any rocks. Over the sand spread a very finely sifted layer of red soil to a depth of 1.5 centimeters, and over that a layer of moss. All in all, the total depth should be six centimeters, bringing it to the top of the flowerbed frame. Pack the earth firmly with a plank. The red earth and the sand can also be mixed and spread as a single layer. Cuttings need a moist environment. A high, dry place is hard to water properly both morning and evening. Next, set up a reed blind at a height of about 1.5 to 2.8 meters to act as a shade for the cuttings. Cut branches to a length of approximately nine to twelve centimeters, and place the cut ends in water to a depth of about six centimeters for six hours. The container should be very clean. If there is the slightest bit of alkalinity in the water, none of the cuttings will root.

The best season for rooting cuttings is from mid-April to mid-June. If the ground cannot be kept moist enough during this period,

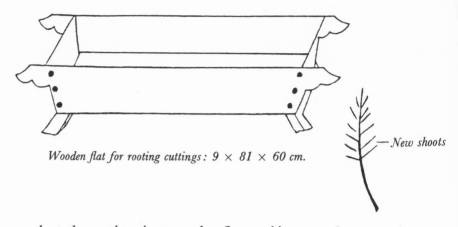

Wooden flat for rooting cuttings: 9 × 81 × 60 cm.

—*New shoots*

plant the cuttings in a wooden flat, making sure there are plenty of drainage holes. Cover the holes with clam shells and fill the flat with the same mixture of earth, sand, red earth, and moss described above. When starting cuttings in a box, follow the same method described earlier. It is worth noting that cuttings should be inserted at an angle rather than straight up. If they are inserted straight, they will be moved by the wind and will not root. A large flat is difficult to move, and a small flat is hard to keep moist. A metal can called a *joro* can be used for watering—it produces a spray resembling light rain, and should be used in the evenings.

Another method of reproduction is the use of softwood or bud cuttings (*mesashi*) made from shoots of the current year. The soil preparation and inserting method for these cuttings is the same as described above. However, the selection of proper cuttings of this type is a secret.

Whatever type of cutting is employed, a sunshade is a must. Transplanting should be done in September and October, and the new plants kept in a warm place over the winter.

Comment: It should be noted that the first type of cutting described is made from old wood and, of course, will require the entire year to root. Until recent times, this was the standard method, and the practice of making summer softwood cuttings is a newer develop-ment. But in China, even today, cuttings of tea (*Camellia sinensis*) are handled in this time-tested manner with a success rate of ninety percent. Camellia cuttings are still rooted in Japan by this method.

Flats are used commonly today when only a few cuttings are being rooted. An apple crate is excellent because it is fairly deep and, when covered with plastic, makes an excellent rooting unit. Furthermore, since it is deep, it can be loosely filled with dry oak leaves for protection in the winter and left out-of-doors until the cuttings are well rooted.

Itō's suggestions for the proper method of making cuttings are precisely those recommended by early English gardeners and are just as useful today. It is interesting that sphagnum is recommended for incorporation into the rooting media, for it is said to be highly sterile. The old Kew gardeners also used to insist on putting the cutting at a slant, even when being inserted in beds inside propaga-ting houses, but probably not for the same reason Itō offers.

Softwood cuttings are now widely employed for azalea reproduc-tion, and the method was probably frequently used in the latter part of the Edo period by experienced growers. It is rather clever of Itō not to disclose his method—but our loss, as we are left hanging with the cuttings only half-prepared. However, his instructions concerning the proper seasons for making cuttings, rooting methods, and the need to provide winter warmth to new cuttings are all well taken.

Manure

Dig up some soil from a sewage canal, dry it well in the sun, and sift finely. This should be mixed with soil in a one-to-three ratio and used for planting.

Alternately, fallen leaves may be buried in the earth, and, when they have decayed to a humuslike texture, dug up and used as a planting medium, again in a one-to-three ratio with soil. This is the best fertilizer of all, and is called *shinobu tsuchi,* or "soil you must

147

wait for." It is good for all plants, but especially so for tsutsuji and satsuki.

Another method is to mix one bucket of human manure with two of water and let it stand in a tub for three weeks to a month, until the odor dissipates. Strain the mixture, and when it rains, pour a little on the roots of the plants, taking care not to get any on the leaves. Never use this unless it is raining; otherwise, it is very harmful. For plants from 30 to 90 centimeters in height, about 1.8 liters is the proper amount. At any rate, if you fertilize too heavily you will harm the plant and the old leaves will drop. March and September are the best months for fertilizing, and summer should be avoided. Fertilize twice a year. No fertilizer is necessary for trees under thirty centimeters in height.

Comment: It is doubtful that either the first or third recommendation would meet current environmental standards or our neighbors' approval. The use of leafmold (as we know *shinobu tsuchi*), however, is as good a recommendation as can be made for azalea cultivation. Itō's prescribed times for fertilization are quite accurate—early spring before growth starts and at the end of the season, when annual growth has been completed.

Postscript

It is the beauty of the view, they say, that makes us, "beneath the cherry blossoms, forget about returning home." In these five volumes the shapes of flowers are illustrated and their colors described so that those who plant tsutsuji can walk among their flower beds and, observing their plants, identify them by name using this book, giving them pleasure even after the blossoms have fallen. As the delights of the four seasons unfold, you will leave behind all troubles and find yourself at peace, and the jeweled tree of the Buddha's enlightenment will take root as you forget, indeed, to return to this fleeting world.

AZALEA LISTS

Tsutsuji

153

Satsuki

Hana Gatami (Flower Keepsake), 115
Hana Kagami (Perfection), 110
Hana Kazura (Flowered Cap), 122
Hana no Moto (Outstanding Flower), 127
Hanazoroe (Galaxy of Flowers), 107
Hatsure Yuki (Patches of Snow), 94
Higurashi (Sunset), 109
Hiroshima Shibori (Tie-dyed Hiroshima), 98
Hitomaru, 123
Hyakuman (One Million), 101

Ichimonji (Number One), 131
Ichiyō (Petal), 108
Ito Kurenai (Crimson Strands), 125

Jūrin (Ten Flowers), 112

Kaguraoka, 116
Kaki Koshimino (Skirted Persimmon Orange), 137
Kappa Koshimino (Skirted Cape), 139
Kashiwazaki, 120
Kashūron (Name obscure), 128
Katsuragi, 102
Katsuyama, 106
Kazaguruma (Windmill), 103
Kii no Kuni, 103
Kiku Mori (Chrysanthemum Grove), 102
Kikyō (Chinese Balloonflower), 104

Kinugawa, 132
Kinshūsan (Brocade Mountain), 107
Kirigane (Beaten Gold), 93
Kiritsubo (Paulownia Court), 129
Kiyo Taki (Clear Waterfall), 111
Kochō (Butterfly), 106
Ko-Fuji (Little Wisteria), 87
Ko-Kin (Small Fortune), 90
Ko-Kurenai (Little Crimson), 96
Ko-Murasaki (Little Purple), 100
Ko-Shibori (Little Tie-dyed), 104
Koshi Nami (Koshi Wave), 100
Kōshoku (Crimson), 86
Ko-Tsubaki (Little Camellia), 121
Kōya Kurenai (Mt. Kōya Crimson), 94
Ko-Zarashi (Little Bleached), 89

Magaki (Hedge), 85
Maki Ginu (Silk Roll), 129
Man'e (Anemone), 95
Matsunami (Pine Wave), 135
Matsushima, 84
Matsushima Koshimino (Skirted Matsushima), 136
Meigetsu (Harvest Moon), 98
Miidera, 110
Mikawa Murasaki (Mikawa Purple), 104
Mine no Yuki (Snow on the Peak), 126
Moku Shibori (Wood-grain Tie-dyed), 125
Momiji Kasane (Layered Maple), 131
Momi Kurenai (Crimson Silk), 86
Muji Shiro (Solid White), 103

Species in Cultivation

I. Azaleas

The following is a list of the species described in *A Brocade Pillow* and their modern Japanese names. It should be noted that the modern names are sometimes different from those used in Itō's day.

SCIENTIFIC NAME	MODERN JAPANESE NAME
Rhododendron dilatatum	Mitsuba tsutsuji
R. eriocarpum	Maruba tsutsuji
R. indicum	Satsuki
R. japonicum	Renge tsutsuji
R. kaempferi	Yama tsutsuji
R. kiusianum	Miyama Kirishima tsutsuji
R. komiyamae	Ashitaka tsutsuji
R. macrosepalum	Mochi tsutsuji
R. x *mucronatum*	Ryukyu tsutsuji
R. ripense	Kishi tsutsuji
R. sataense	Sata tsutsuji
R. scabrum	Kerama tsutsuji
R. schlippenbachii	Kurofune tsutsuji
R. serpyllifolium	Unzen tsutsuji
R. simsii	Tōsatsuki tsutsuji
R. tosaense	Fuji tsutsuji
R. tschonoskii	Kome tsutsuji
R. yedoense	Yodogawa
R. yedoense var. *poukhanense*	Chōsen Yama tsutsuji

II. Other Species

Daphne odora	Jinchōge
Enkianthus campanulatus	Fūrin tsutsuji
Menziesia ciliicalyx	Usugi yōraku

Selected Reading

Many of the following references are now out of print (OP), but most are available in a facsimile edition through a private reprinting service, Theophrastus Reprints, P.O. Box 458, Little Compton, Rhode Island 02837. New editions of several are in the process of being prepared and are noted as such.

Bartlett, H.H., and H. Shohara. 1961. "Japanese Botany during the Period of Wood-Block Printing." *The ASA Gray Bulletin*, n.s. 3, 3–4: 289–561.

Boehmer, L. 1903. *Catalogue of Japanese Plants, Bulbs, and Seeds.* Yokohama. A copy is in the Smithsonian Institution Rare Book Collection.

Lee, Frederick P. 1965. *The Azalea Book.* Second edition. Princeton: D. Van Nostrand. OP. A revised edition is in preparation, but reprints are also available.

Morrison, B.Y. 1953. *The Glenn Dale Azaleas.* Agri. Monogr. No. 20. Washington, D.C.: United States Department of Agriculture. OP.

Ohwi, J. 1965. *Flora of Japan.* Washington, D.C.: Smithsonian Institution.

Sansom, G. 1963. *A History of Japan, 1615–1867.* Stanford: Stanford University Press.

Shirai, M. 1926. "A Brief History of Botany in Old Japan, Past and Present." In *Scientific Japan: Past and Present.* Tokyo: Third Pan-Pacific Science Congress. Chapter 10: 213–27.

Wilson, E.H., and A. Rehder. 1921. *A Monograph of Azaleas.* Cambridge: Cambridge University Press. OP.

The "weathermark" identifies this book as a production of John Weatherhill, Inc., publishers of fine books on Asia and the Pacific. Supervising editor: Jeffrey Hunter. Book design and typography: Miriam Yamaguchi. Production supervision: Yutaka Shimoji. Layout of illustrations: Shinji Moriyama. Composition of text: Korea Textbook, Seoul. Printing of text and engraving and printing of plates, in four-color and monochrome offset: Kinmei Printing, Tokyo. Binding: Okamoto Binderies, Tokyo. The typeface used is Monotype Baskerville.